D1570667

THE MIND OF PLATO

THE MIND OF PLATO

(originally PLATO)

by A. E. TAYLOR

First American Edition

ANN ARBOR PAPERBACKS
The University of Michigan Press

First edition as an Ann Arbor Paperback 1960

First published in 1922 by Constable and Company Ltd.
Published in the United States of America by
The University of Michigan Press and simultaneously
in Toronto, Canada, by Ambassador Books Limited

Manufactured in the United States of America

FOREWORD

The following sketch makes no claim to be considered as a complete account of the philosophy of Plato. Many topics of importance have been omitted altogether, and others only treated with the utmost attainable brevity. I have also thought it necessary to avoid, as far as possible, all controversial discussion, and have therefore in many cases followed my own judgment on disputable points without attempting to support it by the detailed reasoning which would be indispensable in a work of larger scope. My object has been to sit as loose as possible to all the traditional expositions of Platonism, and to give in broad outline the personal impression of the philosopher's thought which I have derived from repeated study of the Platonic text.

Those who are the most competent to condemn the numerous defects of my little book will, I hope, be also most indulgent in their verdict on an attempt to compress into so small a compass an account of the most original and influential of all philosophies.

A.E.T.

CONTENTS

PLATO

CHAPTER I

LIFE AND WRITINGS

THE traditional story of the life of Plato is one in which it is unusually difficult to distinguish between historical fact and romantic fiction. Of the 'Lives' of Plato which have come down to us from ancient times, the earliest in date is that of the African rhetorician and romance-writer Apuleius, who belongs to the middle and later half of the second century A.D. There is a longer biography in the scrap-book commonly known as the *Lives of the Philosophers* by Diogenes of Laerte, a compilation which dates, in its present form, from a time not long before the middle of the third century A.D., though much of its material is taken from earlier and better sources. The remaining 'Lives' belong to the latest age of Neo-Platonism, *i.e.* the sixth century after Christ and later. Thus the earliest extant biography of the philosopher comes to us from a time four hundred years after his death, and must be taken to represent the Platonic legend as it was current in a most uncritical age. When we try to get behind this legend to its basis in well-accredited fact, the results we obtain are singularly meagre. Plato himself has recorded only two facts about his own life. He tells us, in the *Apology*, that he was present in court at the trial of his master Socrates, and that he was one of the friends who offered to be surety for the payment of any fine which might be imposed on the old philosopher. In the *Phaedo* he adds that he was absent from the famous death-scene in the prison, owing to an illness, a statement which may, however, be no more than an artistic literary fiction. His contemporary Xenophon merely mentions him once in passing as a member of the inner Socratic circle. From Aristotle we further learn that Plato, as a young man, apparently before his intimacy with Socrates, had been a pupil of the Heraclitean philosopher Cratylus. A few anecdotes of an unfavourable kind are related by Diogenes of Laerte on the authority of Aristoxenus of Messene, a pupil of Aristotle, and a well-known writer on music, whose credibility is, however, impaired by his unmistakable personal animus against Socrates and Plato, and his anxiety to deny them all philosophical originality. The dates of Plato's birth and death are, moreover, fixed for us by the unimpeachable authority of the Alexandrian chronologists, whose testimony has been preserved by Diogenes. We may thus take it as certain that Plato was born in the year 427 B.C., early in the great Peloponnesian war, and died in 346, at the age of eighty-one. The way in which Xenophon, in his one solitary statement, couples the name of Plato with that of Charmides, a leader of the oligarchy of the 'Thirty,' set up by the Spartans in Athens at the close of the Peloponnesian war, taken together with the prominence given in the Platonic dialogues to Charmides and Critias as friends of Socrates, confirms the later tradition, according to which Plato himself was a near relative of the two 'oligarchs,' a fact which has to be borne in mind in reading his severe strictures upon Athenian democracy.

There remains, indeed, a further source of information, which, if its authenticity could be regarded as established, would be of the very highest value. Among the writings ascribed to Plato and preserved in our ancient manuscripts there is a collection of thirteen letters, purporting to be written by the philosopher himself, some of which ostensibly contain a good deal of autobiographical detail. In particular the seventh letter, the longest and most important of the group, professes to contain the philosopher's own vindication of his life-long abstention from taking part in the public life of his country, and, if genuine, absolutely confirms the later story, presently to be narrated, of his political relations with the court of Syracuse. As to the history of this collection of letters, all that we know for certain is that they were in existence and were regarded as Platonic early in the first century A.D., when they were included by the scholar Thrasyllus in his complete edition of the works of Plato. This, however, is not of itself proof of their genuineness, since the edition of Thrasyllus contained works which we can now show to be spurious, such as the *Theages* and *Erastae*. We further know from Diogenes of Laerte that certain 'letters' had been included in the earlier edition of Plato by the famous scholar Aristophanes, who was librarian of the great museum of Alexandria towards the end of the second century B.C.; but we are not told which or how many of our present collection Aristophanes recognised. When we examine the extant letters themselves, we seem led to the conclusion that they can hardly all be genuine works of Plato, since some of them appear to allude to characteristic doctrines of the Neo-Pythagoreanism which arose about the beginning of the first century before Christ. It is not surprising, therefore, that Grote has stood alone, or almost alone, among recent scholars in maintaining the genuineness of the whole set of thirteen letters admitted into the collection of Thrasyllus. It is another question whether some at least of the collection, and notably the seventh, the only letter of real importance, may not be the work of Plato, and the problem must be said to be one upon which competent scholars are not as yet agreed. On the one side, it may be urged that the incidents related in the seventh letter are in no way incredible, and that their occurrence, as we shall see directly, would explain a certain increase of pessimism in Plato's later writings on political philosophy. On the other, it is suspicious that the letter appears to quote directly from at least four Platonic dialogues (the *Apology*, *Phaedo*, *Republic*, *Lysis*), and that, apart from the account of Plato's relations with Syracuse, it contains nothing which might not have been put together with the help of the dialogues. And we must remember that the desire to exhibit Plato, the great political theorist, actually at work on the attempt to construct a state after his own heart, would at any time have been a sufficient motive for the fabrication. Still, the style of the composition shows that, if a forgery, it is at least an early forgery, and we shall hardly be wrong in treating the narrative as being, at any rate, based upon a trustworthy tradition.

Having premised this much as to the sources of our information, we may now proceed to narrate in outline the biography of Plato, as it was current early in the Christian era, omitting what is evidently myth or mere improving anecdote. Plato, the son of Ariston and Perictione, was born either in Athens or, according to another account, in Aegina, in the year 427 B.C. On the mother's side he was closely related to Critias and Charmides, members of the oligarchy of the 'Thirty,' and the former the leader among its more violent spirits, the family going back through Dropides, a relative of the great lawgiver Solon, to a divine first ancestor, the god Poseidon. On the father's side, too, his origin was no less illustrious, since Ariston was a descendant of Codrus, the last king of Athens, who was himself sprung from Poseidon.

Even this origin, however, was not thought exalted enough for the philosopher by his admirers, and Plato's own nephew, Speusippus, is cited as an authority for the belief that the real father of Perictione's son was the god Apollo. (The relationship between Plato and the family of Critias and Charmides is, as we have said, made probable by the philosopher's own utterances, and he is also himself the authority for the descent of Critias from Dropides. The further assertions about the eminent descent of Dropides are hardly worthy of credit, since it seems clear that Solon the lawgiver was really a middle-class merchant. But the connection with Solon of itself shows that the family was one of the highest distinction as families went in the Athens of the late fifth century.) As a lad, the future philosopher was ambitious of poetical fame, and had even composed a tragedy for public performance. But when he came under the influence of Socrates, he devoted himself entirely to philosophy and burned all his poems. (That so great an imaginative writer as Plato should have begun his literary career as a poet is likely enough, and there is no reason why some of the epigrams ascribed to him in the Greek Anthology should not be genuine, but the story of the burnt tragedy looks like a fabrication based upon the severe condemnation of poetry in general and the drama in particular in the *Republic*; nor must we forget that, according to Aristotle's statement, Plato got his introduction to philosophy not from Socrates, but from Cratylus.) The first association between Plato and Socrates took place when Plato was twenty years old, and their connection lasted eight years, since the death of Socrates falls in 399 B.C. After the death of the master, Plato retired from Athens and spent some years in foreign travel. The accounts of the extent of these travels become more and more exaggerated as the narrators are increasingly removed in date from the actual events. The seventh 'letter' speaks merely of a voyage to Italy and Sicily undertaken apparently in consequence of the writer's disgust with the proceedings of the restored Athenian democracy, which had inaugurated its career by the condemnation of Socrates. Cicero, who is the earliest authority for the story of the travels, apart from the 'letters,' makes Plato go first to Egypt, afterwards to Italy and Sicily. The later Platonic legend professes to know more, and relates an entire romance on the subject of Plato's adventures. According to this story Plato withdrew from

Athens on the death of Socrates, and resided for a while at the neighbouring city of Megara with his friend and fellow-disciple Eucleides. He then visited Cyrene, to enjoy the society of the mathematician Theodorus, Egypt, where he learned the wisdom of the priests, and Italy, where he associated with the members of the Pythagorean school who had survived the forcible dissolution of the political power of the sect. (The tale ran that he further purposed to visit the Persian Magi, but that this scheme failed, though some writers professed to know that Plato had met with Magians and learned their doctrines in Phœnicia.) From Italy the legend brings Plato to Sicily, where he is said, on the authority of the seventh letter, to have arrived at the age of forty; *i.e.* after twelve years of continuous travel. Here he visited the court of the vigorous ruler of Syracuse, Dionysius I., and so displeased that arbitrary monarch by his freedoms of speech that he caused him to be kidnapped by a Spartan ambassador who put him up for sale in the slave-market of Aegina, where, by a singular coincidence, the people had passed a resolution that the first Athenian who should land on the island should be put to death. Plato was, however, saved from his danger by a man of Cyrene, who ransomed him and sent him home to Athens. (How much truth there may be in this story, the details of which are differently given by the different narrators, it is impossible to say with certainty. The story of the kidnapping, in particular, is told with a good deal of discrepancy in the details; many features of it are highly singular, and it appears entirely unknown to both Cicero and the writer of the seventh 'letter.' Hence there is every ground to regard it as pure romance. The same must be said of the story of the twelve years' unbroken travel, and the association of Plato with Oriental priests and magicians. Stories of this kind were widely circulated from the beginning of the first century before Christ onward, when the gradual intermingling of East and West in great cities like Alexandria had given rise to the fancy that Greek science and philosophy had been originally borrowed from Oriental theosophy, a notion invented by Alexandrian Neo-Pythagoreans and eagerly accepted by Jews and Christians, whom it enabled to represent the Greek sages as mere pilferers from the Hebrew scriptures. Even the alleged residence in Megara and the voyage to Cyrene, may be no more than inventions based on the facts that the dialogue *Theaetetus* is dedicated to Plato's friend Eucleides of Megara and that the Cyrenian mathematician Theodorus is one of its *dramatis personae.* So again the frequent allusions in the dialogues to Egypt and Egyptian customs *may* be due to reminiscences of actual travel in Egypt, but can hardly be said to show more knowledge than an Athenian might have acquired at home by reading Herodotus and conversing with traders from the Nile Delta. On the other hand, the story of the visit to Italy and Sicily is confirmed by the fact that Plato's works, as is well known, show considerable familiarity both with Pythagorean science and with the Pythagorean and Orphic theological ideas, and that the first dialogue in which this influence is particularly noticeable is the *Gorgias,* the work in which, as is now generally recognised, Plato speaks for the first time in the tone of the head of a philosophical school or sect. It is thus probable that Plato's final settlement at Athens as a philosophical teacher was actually preceded, as the tradition dating at least from the seventh 'letter' asserts, by a visit to the home of Pythagoreanism, the Greek cities of Sicily and Southern Italy.)

We have to think of Plato, then, as definitely established, from about 387 B.C., in Athens as the recognised head of a permanent seat of learning, a university, as we might call it in our modern terminology. The home of this institution was in the north-western suburb of Athens known as the Academy, in consequence of the presence there of a shrine of the local hero Academus. Here Plato possessed a small property, which was perhaps (the words of the legend as preserved by Diogenes are obscure,) purchased for him by his foreign friends. From this circumstance the philosophical school founded by Plato came to be known in later days as the 'Academy.' It was not the first institution of the kind; Plato's contemporary and rival, the rhetorician and publicist Isocrates, had already gathered round him a similar group of students, and the writings of both authors bear traces of the rivalry between them. Their educational aims were, in fact, markedly different. Isocrates desired, first and foremost, to turn out accomplished and capable men of action, successful orators and politicians. Plato, on the other hand, was convinced that though the trained intelligence ought to direct the course of public life in a well-ordered society, the equipment requisite for such a task must first be obtained by a thorough mastery of the principles of science and philosophy, and was not to be derived from any superficial education in 'general culture.' Thus, while Plato, in well-known passages, describes the pupils of Isocrates as 'smatterers' and 'pretenders to philosophy,' Isocrates, on his side, depreciates those of Plato as unpractical theorists. Of the precise nature of the teaching in Plato's Academy, unfortunately, little is known, but the reports of later tradition, such as they are, indicate that the author of the *Republic* carried his theories of education into practice, and made the thorough and systematic study of exact mathematical science the foundation of all further philosophic instruction. The story that the door of the Academy bore the inscription 'Let none unversed in geometry come under this roof,' is, indeed, first found in the works of a mediæval Byzantine, but its spirit is thoroughly Platonic.

The outward peculiarity, it must be remembered, by which the education given by both Plato and Isocrates differed from that afforded by the eminent 'sophists' of the last half of the fifth century, was that their teaching was more continuous, and that it was, in theory at least, gratuitous. The great sophist of the past had usually been a distinguished foreigner whose task of making his pupils 'good men, able to manage their own private affairs and the affairs of the nation well,' had to be accomplished in the course of a flying visit of a few weeks or months, and he had also been a professional educator, depending upon his professional fees for his livelihood, and therefore inevitably exposed to the temptation to make his instruction attractive and popular, rather than thorough. Plato and Isocrates, on the other hand, were the heads of permanent schools, in which the education of the pupil could be steadily carried on for a protracted period, and where he could remain long after his time of pupilage proper was over, as an associate in the studies of his master. They were, moreover, not dependent for subsistence upon payments by their pupils, and were hence free from the necessity to make their teaching popular in the bad sense of the term, though it is only fair to add that neither had any objection to the occasional reception of presents from friends or pupils, and that Isocrates, at least, required a fee from *foreign* students. It is in virtue of this permanent and organised pursuit of intellectual studies, and this absence of 'professionalism' from their teaching, that we may call Plato and Isocrates the joint creators of the idea of what we now understand by university education. The remark I have just made about the absence of 'professionalism' from their scheme of instruction will, I hope, explain that persistent objection to the sophists' practice of demanding a fee for their courses which Grote found so unreasonable on the part of Plato and Aristotle.

Plato's long life of quiet absorption in his self-chosen task as a director of scientific studies and a writer on philosophy, was destined to be once at least disastrously interrupted. The details of his abortive attempt to put his theories of government into practice at Syracuse must be sought in the histories of Greece. Here it must suffice to recapitulate the leading facts, as related in the 'letters,' and, apparently without any other authority than the 'letters,' in Plutarch's life of Dion. In the year 367 B.C., when Plato was a man of sixty and had presided over the Academy for twenty years, Dionysius I. of Syracuse died, leaving his kingdom to his son Dionysius II., a weak but impressionable youth. The actual direction of affairs was, at the time, mostly in the hands of Dion, the brother-in-law of Dionysius I. and an old friend and admirer of Plato. Plato himself had written in his *Republic* that truly good government will only be possible when a king becomes a philosopher, or a philosopher a king, *i.e.* when the knowledge of sound principles of government and the power to embody them in fact are united in the same person. Dion seems to have thought that the circumstances at Syracuse offered a favourable opportunity for the realisation of this ideal. Why should not Dionysius, under the instructions of the great master, become the promised philosopher-king, and employ the unlimited power at his command to convert Syracuse into something not far removed from the ideal state of Plato's dream? To us, such a project seems chimerical enough, but, as Professor Bury has properly reminded us, the universal belief of Hellas was that a not very dissimilar task had actually been achieved by Lycurgus for Sparta, and there was no *à priori* reason for doubting that what Lycurgus had done for Sparta could be done for Syracuse by Plato. Plato was accordingly invited to Syracuse to undertake the education of the young prince. His reception was, at first, most promising, but the thoroughness with which he set about accomplishing his work foredoomed it to failure. It was the first principle of his political system that nothing but the most thorough training of intelligence in the ideas and methods of science will ever fit a man for the work of governing mankind with true insight. Accordingly he insisted upon beginning by putting his pupil through a thorough course of geometry. Dionysius, naturally enough, soon grew weary of this preliminary drill, and began to revolt against the control of his preceptors. An opportunity was found for banishing Dion, and though Dionysius would have liked to keep Plato with him, the philosopher recognised that his scheme had failed, and speedily pressed for permission to return to Athens. A year or two later he paid another visit to Syracuse, apparently in the hope of reconciling Dion and Dionysius, but without result. The sequel of the story, the rapid development of Dionysius into a reckless tyrant, the expedition of Dion which led to the downfall and flight of Dionysius, the assassination of Dion by Callippus, another pupil of Plato, who then set himself up as tyrant, but was speedily overthrown in his turn by the half-brother of Dionysius, belongs to the history of Sicily, not to the biography of Plato. It is not unlikely that the disastrous failure of the Syracusan enterprise, and the discredit which subsequent events cast upon the members of the Academy, have much to do with the relatively disillusioned and pessimistic tone of Plato's political utterances in the *Theaetetus* and *Politicus* as contrasted with the serenity and hopeful spirit of the greater part of the *Republic.* Yet, even in his old age, Plato seems to have clung to the belief that the experiment which had failed at Syracuse might be successful elsewhere. In his latest work, the *Laws,* which was possibly not circulated until after his death, he still insists that the one chance for the establishment of a really sound form of government lies in the association of a young and high-spirited prince with a wise lawgiver.

Nothing is recorded of the life of Plato after his last return from Syracuse, except that he died —legend says at a wedding-feast—in the year 347-6, at the age of eighty-one. His will, which is preserved by Diogenes, and is likely enough to be genuine, provides for a 'child Adeimantus,' who was probably a relative, as the same name had been borne by one of his half-brothers. Nothing further is known which throws any light on the question whether Plato was ever married or left any descendants. The scurrilous gossip collected by writers like Athenaeus, and the late Neo-Platonic traditions which make him into a celibate ascetic, are equally worthless. The headship of the Academy passed first for a few years to Speusippus, a nephew of Plato, and then to Xenocrates of Chalcedon, another of the master's immediate pupils. The one man of real genius among the disciples, Aristotle of Stageira, took an independent course. For ten or eleven years after the death of the master, of whose school he had been a member from about 367-6 B.C. until 346, he was absent from Athens, being employed for part of the period (343-336 B.C.) as tutor to the future Alexander the Great, then Crown Prince of Macedonia. On his return in 335 he broke away from the Academy, and organised a new school with himself as its head. The formal reverence which Aristotle expresses in his writings for his predecessor was combined with a pugnacious determination to find him in the wrong on every possible occasion. Yet, in spite of the carping and unpleasantly self-satisfied tone of most of the Aristotelian criticism of Plato, the thought of the later philosopher on all the ultimate issues of speculation is little more than an echo of the larger utterance of his master, and it is perhaps as much by inspiring the doctrine of Aristotle as by his own utterances that Plato has continued to our own day to exercise an influence in every department of philosophic thought, which is not less potent for being most often unsuspected. Of the direct and enormously important influence of Platonism on the development of Christian theology this is perhaps hardly the place to speak.

The works of Plato, we have reason to believe, have come down to us absolutely entire and complete. This is, no doubt, to be explained by the fact that the original manuscripts were carefully preserved in the Platonic Academy; thence copies, as Grote has argued, would naturally find their way into the great library at Alexandria. It does not, however, follow that everything which our extant manuscripts of Plato contain must necessarily be Platonic. It would be quite easy, in course of time, for works incorrectly ascribed to Plato, or deliberately forged in his name, to be imposed upon the Alexandrian librarians, and to acquire a standing in the library, side by side with genuine writings derived directly from the original manuscripts preserved at first in the Academy at Athens. Indeed, the very anxiety of the Ptolemies, and their imitators the kings of Pergamus, to make their great collections of books as complete as possible, would furnish a powerful incentive to the unscrupulous to produce alleged copies of works by famous authors. As it happens, we do not know either how long the original manuscripts of Plato continued to exist undispersed (indeed, the very statement that they were kept in the Academy is an inference from the probabilities of the case, and does not rest upon direct ancient testimony), nor what works of Plato were originally included in the Alexandrian library. The first trace which has been preserved of the existence of an edition of Plato in that library is the statement of Diogenes that the scholar Aristophanes of Byzantium made an arrangement of the works of Plato, in which certain of the dialogues were grouped together in 'trilogies,' or sets of three, after the fashion of the tragic dramas of the fifth century. Diogenes gives the names of fourteen dialogues, which, together with a collection of 'letters,' had been thus divided by Aristophanes into five trilogies, and adds that the grouping was not carried out 'for the rest.' Unfortunately, he does not tell us the titles of the 'rest,' so that we have no right to assert that everything now included in our manuscripts was recognised as Platonic at Alexandria in the time of Aristophanes. At a much later date, the grammarian Thrasyllus, who lived in the reigns of Augustus and Tiberius (*i.e.* in the early part of the first century A.D.), made a new classification of the Platonic dialogues into 'tetralogies,' or groups of four, on the analogy of the old tragic tetralogy of three tragedies followed by a satyric play. The Platonic canon of Thrasyllus contained nine of these tetralogies, *i.e.* thirty-five dialogues with a collection of thirteen 'letters,' the same as those we now possess. Of works improperly ascribed to Plato he reckoned ten, five of which are still extant.

No one now supposes that anything which was rejected by Thrasyllus is a genuine work of Plato, but there has been during the last sixty years a good deal of discussion as to whether all that was included by Thrasyllus may safely be accepted. The extreme view that nothing contained in the canon of Thrasyllus is spurious has found no important defender except Grote, whose reasoning is vitiated by the double assumption that everything accepted as genuine by Thrasyllus must have been guaranteed by the Alexandrian library, and that the Alexandrian librarians themselves cannot have been misled or imposed upon. On the other hand, the scepticism of those German critics of the last half of the nineteenth century, who rejected as spurious many of the most important dialogues, including, in some instances, works (*e.g.* the *Laws*) which are specifically named as Plato's by Aristotle, has proved itself even more untenable. Our surest guide in the matter, wherever obtainable, is the evidence of Aristotle, and an increasingly careful study of the Aristotelian text has now enabled us to say that, though some of the chief dialogues are never actually cited by Aristotle in express words, there is none of them, with the doubtful exception of the *Parmenides*, which is not alluded to by him in a way in which, so far as we can discern, he never makes use of any works except those of Plato. There is thus at present a general agreement among scholars that no considerable work in the canon of Thrasyllus is spurious. The few dialogues of his list which are either certainly or possibly spurious are all of them, from the philosophical point of view, insignificant, and no difference is made to our conception of Platonism by our judgment upon them.

A more important question than that of the genuineness or spuriousness of the few minor dialogues about which it is still permissible to doubt is presented by the problem of the order of composition of the leading dialogues. Until some conclusion has been established as to the order in which Plato's principal works were composed, it is impossible to form any intelligible theory of the development of Plato's thought. Now it so happens that the only positive piece of information on this point which has come down to us from antiquity, is the statement of Aristotle that the *Laws* was a later work than the *Republic.* The dialogues themselves enable us to supplement this statement to a slight extent. Thus the *Sophistes* and *Politicus* are expressly represented as continuations of the conversation contained in the *Theaetetus,* and must therefore be later than that dialogue, and for a similar reason the *Timaeus* must be later than the earlier books of the *Republic,* since it recapitulates in its opening the political and educational theories of *Republic* ii.-v. And further, a dialogue which quotes from another, as the *Republic* appears to do from the *Phaedo,* and the *Phaedo* from the *Meno,* must, of course, be later than the dialogue quoted. But the results which can be won by considerations of this kind carry us only a little way, and, in the main, students of Plato were until forty years ago about as devoid of the means of forming a correct conception of the development of Plato's thought as students of Kant would have been of the means of writing the history of Kantianism, if the works of Kant had come down to us entirely undated. Each scholar had his own theory of the order of the dialogues, founded upon some fanciful principle of arrangement for which no convincing grounds could be given. The first step towards the definite solution of the problem by rational methods was taken by Professor Lewis Campbell in 1867 in his edition of the *Sophistes* and *Politicus.* Starting from the universally recognised fact that the *Laws* must, on linguistic grounds, as well as on the strength of ancient tradition, be regarded as Plato's latest composition, Professor Campbell proposed to treat the amount of stylistic resemblance between a given dialogue and the *Laws*, as ascertained by minute linguistic statistics, as a criterion of relative date. The method of investigation thus pointed out has been since followed by a number of other scholars, and notably, and with the greatest wealth of detail, by W. Lutoslawski in his work on *The Origin and Growth of Plato's Logic.* At the same time, much additional light has been thrown on the subject by the more careful investigation of the numerous half-concealed polemical references in Plato to Isocrates, and in Isocrates to Plato. The result is that while we are still by no means able to arrange the works of Plato in an absolutely certain serial order, there is, in spite of some individual points of disagreement, a growing consensus among scholars as to the relative order of succession of the principal dialogues. For a full account of the methods just referred to and the results to which they lead, the reader may be referred to the recent work of Hans Raeder, *Platon's Philosophische Entwickelung*. I shall content myself here with a statement of what appear to be the main results.

Plato's genuine writings fall on examination into four main classes. These are: (1) Early dialogues, marked by the freshness of the dramatic portraiture, the predominant preoccupation with questions of ethics, and the absence of the great characteristic Platonic psychological, epistemological, and metaphysical conceptions, particularly of the famous theory of 'Ideas.' To this group belong the dialogues which have often been called *par excellence* 'Socratic,' such as the *Apology*, *Crito*, *Charmides*, *Laches*, *Euthyphro*, *Euthydemus*, and probably *Cratylus*. The most important members of the group are the *Protagoras* and *Gorgias*, the latter being almost certainly the last of the series. There is reason, as already said, to regard the *Gorgias* as probably composed soon after 387, when Plato was beginning his career as president of the Academy. (2) A group of great dialogues in which Plato's literary power is at its height, and which are all marked by the central position given in them to the 'theory of Ideas,' with its corollary, the doctrine that scientific knowledge is recollection. The *Meno* appears to furnish the connecting link between this group and the preceding; the other members of it are the *Symposium, Phaedo, Republic, Phaedrus.* Of these the *Phaedrus* has been shown, conclusively as I think, by Raeder, and, on independent grounds, by Lutoslawski, to be later than the *Republic,* which, in its turn, is pretty certainly later than the other two. Since the *Phaedrus* appears to allude to the *Panegyricus* of Isocrates, which was published in 380 B.C., the 'second period' of Plato's activity as a writer must have extended *at least* down to that year. (3) A group of dialogues of a 'dialectical' kind, in which the primary objects of consideration are logical questions, the nature of true and of false predication, the problem of the categories, the meaning of negation, the processes of logical division and definition. An external link is provided between the dialogues of this group by the exceptional prominence given in them all to the doctrines of the great Eleatic philosopher Parmenides. The group consists of four great dialogues, *Theaetetus, Parmenides, Sophistes, Politicus.* The last two are undoubtedly later than the others. They are, in form, continuations of the conversation begun in the *Theaetetus*, and are shown to be later than the *Parmenides* both by linguistic evidence and by the presence in the *Sophistes* of an explicit allusion to the arguments of the *Parmenides*. Whether the *Theaetetus* is also later than the *Parmenides* is still an open question, though it also contains what looks like a distinct reference to that dialogue.

(4) Three important works remain which form, linguistically, a group by themselves and must be referred to the latest years of Plato's life: the *Philebus*, the maturest exposition of Platonic ethics; the *Timaeus* (with its fragmentary continuation, the *Critias*), concerned in the main with cosmology and physics, but including a great deal that is of high metaphysical and ethical importance; and the *Laws*, in which the aged philosopher, without abandoning the ideals of the *Republic*, undertakes the construction of such a 'second-best' form of society as might be actually practicable not for 'philosophers,' but for average fourth-century Greeks. Actual dates can hardly be determined in connection with these two last groups. We can only say that the seven works mentioned must have been written between 380 (the earliest possible date for the *Phaedrus*) and

347-6, the year of Plato's death, and that the difference of tone between the third and second groups of dialogues makes it almost certain that the earliest works of the third group fall at least some years later than the *Phaedrus*. It is tempting to go a step further, and say, with Lutoslawski, that the bitter expressions of the *Theaetetus* about the helplessness of the philosopher in practical affairs contain a personal allusion to the failure of Plato's own intervention at Syracuse, in which case the *Theaetetus* and all the following dialogues must be later than 367-6, but the inference is far from certain.

This chapter may conveniently end with some brief observations on the form of the Platonic writings, and the difficulties which that form creates for the interpreter of Plato's thought. In form, the philosophical works of Plato are all dramatic; they are, one and all, διάλογοι, conversations. This is true even of the *Apology*, which is, in point of fact, no set speech, but a series of colloquies of Socrates with his accuser and his judges. It is true that the dramatic element becomes less prominent as we pass from the earlier works to the later. In the dialogues of our last two groups, the function of the minor personages becomes less and less important.

They tend, more and more, to serve as mere instruments for giving the chief speaker his cue, until in the *Timaeus* the conversation becomes a mere prelude to the delivery of a consecutive and unbroken cosmological discourse, and in the *Laws* the two minor characters have little more to do than to receive the instructions of their companion with appropriate expressions of agreement. We note, too, that in general the position of chief speaker is assigned to Socrates, though in three of the later dialogues (the *Sophistes*, *Politicus*, and *Timaeus*) he recedes into the background, as though Plato felt that he was passing in these works definitely beyond the bounds of the Socratic influence, while in the *Laws* he disappears altogether (probably because the scene of the dialogue is laid in Crete, where the introduction of the home-keeping son of Sophroniscus would have been incongruous), and his place is taken by a 'stranger from Athens,' who is palpably no other than Plato himself. Plato's reasons for choosing the dialogue as the most appropriate vehicle of philosophical thought are not hard to discover. It was the natural mode of expression for a philosophic movement which originated in the searching and incisive conversation of Socrates. Most of the 'Socratic men' expressed their ideas in the guise of Socratic dialogue, and Plato may not have been the originator of the practice. Moreover, Plato, as he himself tells us, had a poor opinion of written books as provocative of thought, in comparison with the actual face-to-face discussion of problems and examination of difficulties between independent seekers for truth. The dialogue form recommended itself to him as the nearest literary approximation to the actual contact of mind with mind; it enabled him to examine a doctrine successively from the points of view of its adherents and its opponents, and thus to ensure thoroughness in the quest for truth. And finally, the dialogue, more than any other form of composition, gives full play to the dramatic gifts of portrayal of character and humorous satire in which Plato takes rank with the greatest comic and tragic masters. At the same time, Plato's choice of the dialogue as his mode of expression has created a source of fallacy for his interpreters. If we would avoid serious errors, it is necessary always to remember that the personages of one of Plato's philosophical dialogues are one and all characters in a play. 'Protagoras' or 'Gorgias,' in a Platonic dialogue, is not the historical Professor of that name, but a fictitious personage created by

Plato as a representative of views and tendencies which he wishes to criticise. Mingled with traits drawn from the actual persons whose names these characters bear, we can often find in the picture others which can be known or suspected to belong to the writer's contemporaries. And the same thing is true, though the fact is commonly forgotten, of the protagonist of the drama, the Platonic 'Socrates.' 'Socrates' in Plato is neither, as some of the older and more uncritical expositors used to assume, the historical Socrates, nor, as is too often taken for granted to-day, the historical Plato, but the hero of the Platonic drama. The hero's character is largely modelled on that of the actual Socrates, his opinions are often those of the historical Plato, but he is still distinct from them both. In particular, it is a grave mistake of interpretation to assume that a proposition put forward by 'Socrates' must necessarily represent the views of his creator, or that where 'Socrates' declares himself baffled by a problem, Plato must always have been equally at a loss. Plato shares to the full that gift of Attic 'irony' which is so characteristic of the great Athenian tragedians, and, as any attentive reading of the *Protagoras* will show, he has no objection to exercising it, on occasion, at the expense of his principal personage. In determining which of the views of his hero are put forward as his own, we, who are deprived of the oral instructions dispensed to the students of the Academy, have to observe much the same conditions and practise much the same precautions as are required for similar interpretation of a great dramatist or novelist.

CHAPTER II

KNOWLEDGE AND ITS OBJECTS

THE word 'philosophy,' which to us has come to mean no more than a body of theories and inquiries, has for Plato a more living and subjective sense. Philosophy is, as its name declares, the *love* of wisdom, the passionate striving after truth and light which is, in some degree, the dower of every human soul. It belongs, the *Symposium* tells us, neither to the mind that is wholly wise, nor to that which is merely and complacently stupid. It is the aspiration of the partly illuminated, partly confused and perplexed, soul towards a complete vision in which its present doubts and difficulties may vanish. According to the *Theaetetus* and *Republic*, philosophy begins in wonder, or more precisely in the mental distress we feel when confronted by conflicting perceptions, each apparently equally well accredited. In a famous passage this state of distress, in which the soul is, so to say, in travail with a half-formed idea, is likened to the pains of child-birth, and the philosopher is presented, in his relation to his disciples, as the midwife of the spirit. His task is not to think for other men, but to help them to bring their own thoughts to the birth. This conception of philosophy and its function is far from being narrowly 'intellectualist' in a bad sense. Philosophy is, in Plato's eyes, a 'way of life,' a discipline for character no less than for understanding. But it is his conviction that there is a deep truth enshrined in the crude saying of the old physiologists that 'like is known by like.' His theory of education is dominated by the thought that the mind itself inevitably 'imitates' the character of the things it habitually contemplates. Just because the aspiration after wisdom is the fundamental expression of the mind's true nature, it cannot be followed persistently without resulting in a transfiguration of our whole character; its ultimate effect is to reproduce in the individual soul those very features of law, order, and rational purpose which the philosopher's contemplation reveals as omnipresent in the world of genuine knowledge. Yet the starting-point of the whole process is an intellectual emotion, a passion for insight into truth. The upward pilgrimage of the soul begins for Plato not, as for Bunyan, with 'conviction of sin,' but with that humiliating sense of ignorance which Socrates aimed at producing in those who submitted to his cross-questioning. Insight and enlightenment are the first requisites for sound morality, no less than for science. In action as well as in speculation, what distinguishes the 'philosopher' from other men is the fact that where they have mere 'opinions' he has 'knowledge,' *i.e.* convictions which have been won by free intellectual inquiry and can be justified at the bar of reason.

The 'theory of knowledge' is thus the very centre of Plato's philosophy. He takes his stand upon the fundamental assumption that there really is such a thing as 'science,' *i.e.* as a body of knowable truth which is valid always and absolutely and for every thinking mind. The problem he sets before himself in his metaphysics is to find the answer to the question 'How is science possible?' 'What is the general character which must be ascribed to the objects of our scientific knowledge?' Plato may, therefore, in spite of Kant's hasty inclusion of him among the dogmatists, be truly said to be a great 'critical' philosopher, and, indeed, with a partial reservation in favour of his revered predecessor Parmenides, the earliest critical philosopher of Europe. Indeed, it is not too much to say that Plato's fundamental problem is essentially identical with that of Kant in the *Critique of Pure Reason,* though Plato's solution of it differs strikingly in some respects from Kant's. Like Kant, he finds his point of departure in the broad contrast between the world of everyday unsystematised 'experience,' and that of science. The world as it appears to the everyday unscientific man is a scene of strange disorder and confusion; his so-called experience is made up of what Plato calls 'opinions,' a multitude of conflicting and changing beliefs, some of which are often actually contradictory of others; he can give no satisfactory grounds for regarding them as true, and can often be persuaded out of them by appeals to irrational emotion. Science, on the other hand, is a body of consistent and fixed convictions, a system of truths, valid absolutely, always, and for every one, in which the various members are connected by a bond of logical necessity—in a word, a body of reasoned deductions from true principles. What then is the relation between these apparently so diverse worlds, that of 'opinion' and that of 'science'? In more modern language, of what nature are the objects cognised by the universal propositions of science, and how are they related to the particular percepts of sense? Plato's answer to this question is contained in his famous 'Theory of Ideas,' which is thus, according to its author's intention, neither 'dogmatic' metaphysics nor poetical imagery, but a logical doctrine of the import of universal propositions.

The real character of this central Platonic doctrine, as primarily a theory of predication, is well brought out by the succinct account of its meaning and its logical connection with previous Greek thought given by Aristotle in his *Metaphysics.* According to Aristotle, the doctrine was a logical consequence from two premises, taken one from Heracliteanism, the other from Socrates. From Heracliteanism Plato had learned that all the kinds of things which our senses perceive are 'in flux,' *i.e.* are constantly undergoing all sorts of incalculable changes, and consequently that no universal truths can be formulated about them. (*Cf.* Locke's doctrine that all our certain knowledge of 'nature' is 'barely particular.') From Socrates, whose methods, though used by himself only in the discussion of 'matters of conduct,' were really of universal application, he further learned that without universal truths there can be no science. Hence, since there is such a thing as science, Plato inferred that the objects which science defines, and about which she undertakes to prove universally valid conclusions, cannot be the indefinitely variable things of the sensible physical world. There is therefore a supra-physical world of entities, eternal and immutable, and it is these unchanging entities, called by Plato 'Ideas,' which are the objects with which the definitions and universal truths of exact science are concerned. The relation between this world of pure logical concepts and the world of every-day sensible experience is that the things of the sensible world are approximate and imperfect resemblances of the corresponding conceptual entities from which they get their various class-names. This relation Plato calls 'participation in' the Ideas, a phrase to which Aristotle objects that it is no more than a misleading imaginative metaphor. Such is the preliminary account which Aristotle prefixes to his 'smashing' attack on the Platonic metaphysics.

When we turn to the great dialogues, such as the *Phaedo, Republic, Timaeus,* in which the doctrine of Ideas is most prominent, we find this account, so far as it goes, fully borne out. In the *Timaeus,* in the only passage where Plato ever directly raises the question whether the 'Ideas' actually exist or not, their existence is said to be a necessary implication of the reality of the distinction between 'true opinion' and 'science.' If science is no more than true opinion, there need be no objects except those of the physical and sensible world; if science is other than true opinion, there must be a corresponding difference between objects of which we can only have true opinion and objects of which we can have scientific knowledge. But science is assuredly something more than true opinion; it deals with things which cannot be perceived by the senses, but only conceived by thought; it is eternally and immutably valid; it rests on rational grounds and logical proof. 'Ideas' therefore exist. So again, in the three dialogues alike, we find that there is a standing contrast between the unity of the 'Idea' and the multiplicity of the things which, as Plato puts it, 'participate' in the 'Idea,' or, as we should say, of which the corresponding term can be predicated. There are a countless host of beings whom we call *men* or *oxen*, of things which we speak of as *just* or *beautiful*, but the *humanity* we predicate of one man is identical with the *humanity* we predicate of any other: the *justice* or *beauty* in virtue of which we call different persons or things just or beautiful is always one and the same. Again, a thing or person who is beautiful may become unbeautiful, may cease, in Platonic language, to 'participate in' Beauty, but Beauty itself never begins nor ceases, but simply is eternally identical with itself. And, once more, the pure logical concept is never fully embodied in any sensible example: two things, for instance, which at the first blush appear equal, on closer comparison will be found to be only approximately so; the visible diagram which we take to stand for a triangle, in studying geometry, has never really the properties which we attribute to 'the triangle' in our definition; the conduct we praise as just may, on close scrutiny, turn out to be only imperfectly just. Thus Socrates, ABC, the conduct of an Aristides, 'partake' of humanity, of triangularity, of justice; they are not humanity, triangularity, justice 'themselves.' 'What man is in itself,' 'what justice is in itself,' is always something other than any one man or any one just deed.

Considerations like these show us clearly what is the entity to which Plato gives the name of an 'Idea.' It is what we should now call the 'signification' or 'intension' of a class-name, as distinguished from its 'extension.' The extension of the name is what Plato means when he speaks of the 'many things which partake of' the one Idea or class-concept. Consequently he sometimes says that there exists an Idea for every group of many things which 'have a common name,' and we find Aristotle using the expression 'the One over the Many' as a synonym for the Platonic Idea. But this restriction of the range of Ideas to classes of *many* things with a common class-concept is not really involved in the general theory of the nature of the Idea, since, as the existence of significant singular terms shows us, classes with only one member are just as common in logic as classes with many, and so we find Plato in the *Timaeus* explicitly recognising one such concept or Idea which is 'partaken of' by only one sensible thing, viz. the Idea or concept of the physical universe itself as a whole (the so-called *αὐτοζῷον*). By the 'Ideas,' then, Plato means the system of terms or concepts of fixed and determinate intension which would form the contents of an ideally perfect science, and which form the content of our existing science in so far as it is completely and rigidly 'scientific,' the system of universal meanings. Before we go further, it may be as well to call attention to one or two points in regard to which his doctrine is capable of being and has often actually been misunderstood.

(1) Plato's theory of 'Ideas,' as the true objects of knowledge, is not at all a doctrine of 'Idealism' in the modern sense of the word. He calls the concepts of science 'Ideas' simply because they constitute the forms or types in accordance with which the universe of things is constructed; the words *ἰδέα, εἶδος*, simply mean 'shape,' 'form,' and nothing more. We merely miss his meaning if we allow the Berkeleyan notion of an 'idea' as a state of mind to affect our interpretation of him. The suggestion that an 'Idea' is something which only exists 'in a soul,' and therefore is a 'thought,' is only made once in Plato's writings, in a passage of the *Parmenides,* and is only put forward there to be promptly rejected. With Plato the 'Ideas' are not 'states' of the knowing mind, but objects distinct from and independent of itself, *about* which it has knowledge. It is only with the Neo-Platonists, who taught that 'objects of thought have no subsistence outside the thinking mind,' that we come within measurable distance of any form of modern 'Idealism.' Hence 'conceptual realism' is a much better and less ambiguous name than 'Idealism' for the type of

doctrine of which Plato is the most illustrious exponent.

(2) It follows also at once that, since the 'Ideas' are not processes of thought but objects of thought, we must not conceive of them as the thoughts of the divine mind, 'creative conceptions' of God. This interpretation of Plato is as old, at least, as the Alexandrian Jewish philosopher Philo, a contemporary of Christ, and has found notable support in modern times, but is, none the less, thoroughly un-Platonic. It is not easy to tell how far, when Plato speaks of personal gods or a personal God, he is using the language of exact philosophy, or how far he is merely accommodating himself to the current phraseology of his time; but this much, at least, is clear. When God is spoken of in connection with the 'Ideas,' as in the *Timaeus,* where he is imaginatively portrayed as shaping the physical universe on the model of the 'Ideas,' the 'Ideas' are always referred to as objects existing independently of God and known by Him, never as owing their existence to His thought about them. In fact, whatever may have been Plato's precise conception of God, God appears in the language of the dialogues as altogether secondary in his system; it is the 'Ideas,' and not, as in so many modern

systems, God, which are, for Plato, the *ens realissimum.* As we shall see further in the next chapter, it is just because God and 'the soul' are not for Plato *entia realissima* that he has to employ imaginative myths when he would speak of them, whereas his language, when he deals with the 'Ideas,' is as devoid of mythical traits as the multiplication table.

(3) In speaking of the relation between the members of the extension of a class-name and the common intension or class-concept or 'Idea' which corresponds to them, Plato employs not only the expression, regarded by Aristotle as specially characteristic of him, that the various things 'partake of' the Idea, but a number of equivalent phrases. Thus it is said (*Phaedo*) that the things 'have communion with' (κοινωνεῖ) the Idea, or that the Idea 'is present to' (πάρεστι) them; and it is explicitly declared that it does not matter which of these expressions we use, so long as we understand the relation which they all denote. Yet another way of expressing the same relation is to say that the things are 'imitations' (μιμήματα) or 'copies' of Ideas. This form of expression naturally meets us more particularly in the semi-mythical cosmogony of the *Timaeus*, but it is found also side by side with the language

about 'participation' in the *Republic*; and in the *Parmenides*, where a number of difficulties are being raised about the nature of 'participation,' it is expressly asked whether the 'participation' of things in the Ideas may not be explained more exactly by the view that they are 'likenesses' of them. The same metaphor is, of course, implied in all passages which dwell upon the imperfect and merely approximate character of the embodiment of Ideas in sensible things. Hence it is clear that there is no ground for the recent interpretation which distinguishes between an earlier version of Platonism, according to which things 'participate' in Ideas, and a later version in which they merely 'resemble' them. In fact, as has well been shown by Professor Shorey, the whole conception of a marked difference between an earlier and a later Platonic metaphysic has no tenable foundation. All these different metaphors are intended to express one and the same relation, viz. that which subsists between the subject and predicate of such propositions as 'Socrates *is a* man,' '*ABC is a* triangle,' the relation, that is, between the individual member of a class and the class to which it belongs. The peculiarity of Plato's view is that, whereas modern exact logic treats this relation (denoted in the symbolism of Peano by ε) as a relation between the individual and the *extension* of the class ('Socrates *is a* man' = 'Socrates is one member of the group *men*'), Plato treats it as a relation between the individual and the intension of the class-name ('Socrates *is a* man' = 'Socrates possesses humanity,' or 'humanity is found in Socrates').

(4) From the time of Aristotle to the present day the point which has given rise to the sharpest criticism of Plato has always been his insistence on the 'transcendent' character of the Ideas. This character is expressed in Plato by his reiterated assertion that the Ideas are something 'separate from' (χώρις) the things which 'participate in' or 'resemble' them, and are called by their names. It is upon this point that Aristotle's most incisive attacks upon the Platonic theory turn. He treats Plato's doctrine as amounting to the assertion that, *e.g.* 'humanity' and 'triangularity' are things which exist apart from and outside of all actually existing men or triangles, and objects that, if this is so, there can be no intelligible connection between the supposed world of Ideas and the world of concrete realities. If the Idea is 'outside' or 'apart from' all sensible things, how can it be their inmost reality or 'substance'; and again, how can know-

ledge of Ideas and their relations contribute in any way to our scientific knowledge of the real world? Aristotle thus leads the way in regarding Plato's doctrine as a 'reification of concepts,' a fallacious attribution of substantive existence to universal predicates, and condenses his objection to it in the statement that what science requires is not that there should be 'Ideas, or a One which is something over and above the Many,' but merely that one attribute should be predicable of many subjects. The difficulty has been felt so strongly by modern interpreters that many of them have endeavoured, in the face of Plato's plainest declarations, to explain it away, and thus to bring Plato's theory of predication into accord with that of his great disciple. Plato's language, however, is too explicit to permit of any such interpretation, as Aristotle was well aware. More careful consideration will, I think, both explain its true meaning and throw some light on a probable source of the Platonic theory which Aristotle's analysis leaves only imperfectly indicated. If we consider the passages, from the *Phaedo* onwards, in which Plato insists most strongly on the 'transcendent' and 'separate' character of the Idea and the imperfection of its sensible embodiment, we shall find that his illustrations are drawn from two spheres, those of mathematics and of ethics. It is primarily in mathematics and in ethics that the Idea most obviously appears as an Ideal, a conceptual limit to which experience only presents imperfect approximation. And when we remember the importance attached by Plato to measure, order, and proportion as characteristics of the morally good, we may see reason to reduce the two cases to one. It is primarily from mathematics that Plato has derived his conception of science and its concepts and their relation to the world of experience. Now, as Plato himself reminds us in the *Republic*, the visible diagrams of the mathematician are only aids to the imagination; they are not themselves the true objects of his reasoning. He may represent a point by a visible dot, or a line by a stroke drawn with chalk; but these dots and strokes are not really the points and lines about which he is reasoning, and have not really the properties which he ascribes to the point and the line (*e.g.* the visible dot is not, like the true point, a thing without parts or magnitude; the visible stroke is never devoid of breadth or absolutely straight, and so on). The real objects of mathematical study are a system of pure logical concepts which can be thought with exact precision but cannot be adequately represented to sense or imagination. In Plato's theory of Ideas we have a conception of science which rests upon the view that mathematics is the one and only true science, a consistent working out of the thought expressed by Kant in his saying that every study contains only so much of science as it contains of pure mathematics. That Plato's doctrine of knowledge should thus have arisen primarily from reflection upon the concepts and methods of pure mathematics is in accord not only with the special prominence given both in the dialogues and, so far as we can learn, in the oral teaching of the Academy, to mathematical study, but also with the historical fact that pure mathematics was in Plato's time the only scientific study in which certain and well-established results had been attained.

These same considerations also explain why the answer given by Plato to the question 'How is scientific truth possible?' differs so greatly from the answer given by Kant and his followers to the same problem. For Plato the great Kantian problem 'How is pure *à priori* natural science possible?' does not exist. 'Natural science,' in the sense of proved universal laws of physical process, had for him no being. A true 'science of physical nature' could, of course, not exist in the fourth century B.C., which possessed neither the appliances requisite for precise determination of physical magnitudes nor the mathematical methods necessary for the establishment of general laws on the basis of individual observations. But even had the physics of the twentieth century A.D. been known to Plato, it is pretty clear that he would still have refused to bestow the title of science upon our knowledge of actual nature. He would have called attention to the merely approximate character of all actual physical measurements, and the necessity of admitting that the course of any actual physical process may be influenced by the presence of conditions which are neglected in our formulation of 'general laws of sequence,' in justification of the view that our results are only strictly proved, and therefore rigidly scientific, so long as we confine ourselves within the domains of pure conceptual mathematics. For him the actual physical world, just because it cannot be completely analysed into combinations of logical concepts, but involves a factor of irrational sensible fact, is incapable of being an object of science proper. Any conclusions we may form as to its structure and history must be put forward, not as proved results of science, but as, at best, a 'probable account.' The physical world is thus the proper object of 'opinion,' and any account of its development must be, like the narrative of Timaeus, largely mythical. (Compare once more Locke's doctrine of the extent of our knowledge of 'real existence' of sensible things, and the position of those eminent logicians who hold that 'induction' from observed facts is unable to lead to results which are more than probable.) Hence while Kant denounces all 'transcendent' employment of the fundamental concepts of science, and confines knowledge within the limits of 'possible experience,' Plato, to put the matter quite plainly, holds that all true science is 'transcendent' and deals with objects which lie entirely beyond the range of any possible 'experience' of sense. Where 'experience' begins, science, in his opinion, leaves off. That Kant does not come to the same conclusion seems to be due to his assumption that the sciences of Arithmetic and Geometry deal with objects which are not analysable into purely logical concepts, but involve an element of irrational sensuous 'intuition.' It is this assumption which Plato is really denying by anticipation when he says in the *Republic* that the diagrams of the geometers are mere aids to the imagination, and not themselves the objects of geometrical reasoning, and again in the *Timaeus* that space is apprehended not by sense but by a 'kind of bastard thought.'

We have seen, then, what is the general character of the system of Platonic Ideas, the true object of scientific knowledge. It is a world of exactly defined logical concepts, each standing in immutable relations to the rest. Further light is thrown upon the internal structure of this system by a famous passage at the end of the sixth book of the *Republic*, which, taken along with the exposition of it in the following book, is by far the most important single text for the whole of Plato's epistemology. In this passage Plato is concerned to distinguish four grades of cognition, and to provide each with its appropriate class of objects. He illustrates his meaning by what is, in point of fact, a diagram. He takes a vertical line, and begins by dividing it into an upper and a lower segment, the upper segment representing knowledge or science, the lower 'opinion.' Each segment is then, in turn, once more divided into an upper and a lower part, in the same ratio in which the whole line was originally divided. We thus get an inferior and a superior form of 'opinion' and of knowledge respectively, the inferior, in each case, standing in respect of its truth and certainty to the higher, in the same relation in which 'opinion' as a whole stands to knowledge. The lowest type of cognition of all, the inferior form of 'opinion,' Plato calls εἰκασία, 'guess-work,' with a punning allusion to the εἰκόνες or 'images' which are its appropriate objects. It is the state of mind in which reflections in water and the imagery of dreams are not as yet distinguished from the solid physical realities of which they are the images, the mental condition of the savage or child at the mercy of 'primitive credulity,' who accepts every presentation, so long as it lasts, as equally true with any other, and has not yet learned to know the shadow from the substance. A more developed and truer form of cognition is represented by πίστις, belief, the state of mind of the man who, while still recognising the existence of nothing but the sensible, has learned to distinguish physical things from their mere shadows or reflections or dream-images, and thus to make a distinction between the truth-values of the two kinds of presentation. Such a man, though as yet not possessed of proved and universal scientific truth, has already a fair stock of tolerably systematised and trustworthy convictions about the empirical course of things, and, as we have seen, Plato holds that this is the highest degree of truth which can be attained in the study of the actual physical world. Thus *πίστις* corresponds exactly to what we should call sensible experience, and the knowledge based on induction from such experience. A further step is taken towards the ideal of genuine knowledge when we pass from the higher form of 'opinion' to the lower form of science. Plato's name for this inferior grade of science is *διάνοια*, which we may loosely render 'understanding,' and it is declared to be the knowledge supplied by 'geometry and the kindred arts,' *i.e.* mathematics as usually studied. Being 'science,' these studies have for their object concepts of a purely rational kind, and hence Plato observes that they use diagrams and models, which for 'opinion' are realities as mere images of the higher realities with which they are concerned. But he finds two defects in the procedure of ordinary mathematics: the mathematician employs sensible aids, even if he uses them only as aids to his imagination; he also makes use of a host of notions which he has not defined and postulates which he has not proved. Hence Plato maintains that there must be a still more perfect realisation of the ideal of knowledge, which is given by a science called by him 'dialectic,' which has for its objects 'Ideas' or 'Forms' themselves, and studies them without the aid of any sensuous representations whatever. The procedure of 'dialectic,' as he describes it, is twofold: a process of analysis followed by one of synthesis. The dialectician will start in his turn with the axioms and indefinables of the ordinary mathematician, but he will not regard them as ultimate. He will treat them as literally 'hypotheses,' bases or starting-points from which he may ascend to a supreme first principle which is 'unhypothetical'; then from the cognition of this first principle he will once more descend by a regular gradation to the knowledge of its consequences, proceeding throughout 'from forms to forms without the aid of anything sensible.' That is, it seems, the dialectitian is to compare the principles assumed as ultimate by the various branches of mathematics, and as a result of the comparison to arrive at some still more ultimate first principle of a logical character which is self-evidently true. Having done this, he is then to deduce the supposed ultimates of the ordinary mathematician, and through them their consequences, from his own supreme and self-evident axiom. Only when this has been done shall we have realised the ideal of scientific investigation, the reduction of known truth to a systematic body of logical deductions from true and ultimate premises.

It is clear from this that Plato's conception is closely akin to the ideal of the growing school of mathematicians who maintain that the whole of pure mathematical science is a body of deductions from a few ultimate premises which are all of a purely logical kind, and require for their statement no primary notions except those of formal logic. Could he have met with such a work as the *Formulaire* of Professor Peano, or the *Grundgesetze der Arithmetik* of Professor Frege, he would plainly have felt that his conception of 'dialectic' was there very largely justified and realised. But there are also very important differences between the 'dialectic' of Plato and the 'logistic' of our contemporary philosophical mathematicians. For one thing, Plato, like Leibniz after him, dreamed of the deduction of all pure science from a single ultimate principle, while the development of exact logic has definitely shown that the principles of logic themselves form a body of mutually independent postulates, the number of which the old traditional logic, with its three laws of thought, seriously underestimated. A still more important difference appears when we ask what, in Plato's opinion, is the character of the supreme principle itself. He tells us that it is 'the good' or the 'Idea of the good,' which is to the world of concepts what 'its offspring' the sun is to the sensible world. Now, in the sensible world, the sun has a double function. It is the source of the light by which the eye beholds both the sun itself and everything else; it is also, as the source of heat, the cause of growth and vitality. So, in the world of concepts, the 'good' is at once the source of knowledge and illumination to the knowing mind, and the source of reality and being to the objects of its knowledge. And all the time, just as the sun is not itself light or growth, so the 'good' is not itself Being or Truth, but the transcendent source of both. Plato's meaning in this famous passage is far from easy to grasp with precision, as he himself seems to admit, but his general sense may perhaps be divined by a comparison with well-known passages of other dialogues. There is a famous page of the *Phaedo* which professes, it is hard to say with what degree of accuracy, to trace the mental biography of Socrates. After recounting his youthful dissatisfaction with the mutually conflicting theories of various early physicists about the universe, Socrates is made to say that he hailed with rapture the saying of Anaxagoras that it is Mind which is the cause of order and structure in the universe. This he took to mean that if mind is responsible for the universe, its existing arrangements must be those which are best, and he eagerly procured the book of Anaxagoras in the hope that he would find there a theory of the universe in which every detail would be justified by a proof that it was better for things to be as the writer said than to be in any other way. On reading the work he was, however, disgusted to find that Anaxagoras did not live up to his own principles, but for the most part accounted for existing facts by hypotheses of mechanical causation, only appealing to Mind as the universal cause when he was at a loss for some more specific mechanical explanation of a fact. This criticism of Anaxagoras, in which Aristotle emphatically concurs, is then made the opportunity for drawing an important distinction between the true cause of a thing and subordinate accessory conditions, 'without which the cause would not be a cause.' The true cause of every arrangement in nature is that 'it is best that things should be so';

the alleged mechanical 'causes' of the men of science are merely accessory conditions in the absence of which the efficacy of the true cause would be destroyed. We find this distinction carefully observed in the half-mythical cosmogony of Plato's own *Timaeus*. The true reason or cause of the existence of the universe is the goodness of God, who, being good Himself, desired that His work too should be as good as possible; the accessory conditions are provided for by the character of the disorderly material out of which the universe is moulded by God. Thus we see that for Plato, as for the Greek mind in general, to be *good* means to be good *for* some end or purpose, to be the expression of a rational aim or interest. Evil, on the other hand, is precisely that which is disorderly, which hampers or frustrates the execution of rational purpose. (And hence, by the way, there is, on Plato's principles, an irreducible element of evil in the physical universe, precisely because that universe contains, as the system of pure concepts does not, an irrational and incalculable factor.)

Putting all this together, we may say that the recognition of the 'good,' as the supreme source from which the 'Ideas' derive their being, would appear to mean that the whole body of true scientific concepts forms an organic unity in which each member is connected with the rest teleologically by the fact that some of them point forward, or logically lead up, to it, while it, in its turn, leads up to others. The objective unity of the system of scientific concepts is thus the counterpart of the unity of aim and purpose which it is the mission of philosophy, according to Plato, to bring about in the philosopher's inner life.

In the great series of dialectical dialogues, which we may safely follow the all but unanimous opinion of the latest scholars in regarding as posterior to the *Phaedo-Republic* group, Plato in the main turns away from his original problem of the relation between the individual thing and the intension of the class to which we refer it, to deal with further questions of logic and epistemology. This does not mean, as has sometimes been supposed, that he has abandoned or come to make serious modifications in his doctrine of 'Ideas,' as may be seen both from the reappearance of the familiar theory in the *Timaeus* and from the manifestly *bona fide* ignorance of Aristotle as to any difference in principle between an earlier and a later Platonism. What it means is simply that the whole theory of knowledge is not exhausted for Plato by any single doctrine. It is precisely in this group of dialogues that we find Plato anticipating the achievement of Aristotle in the creation of a scientific logical terminology to a degree which entitles him fairly to be called, rather than any other one man, the creator of logic. In the *Parmenides, Theaetetus,* and *Sophistes* we meet, among other things, the first attempt to construct a table of the categories, or leading scientific conceptions required for the ordering of experience. Plato's list varies slightly according as his immediate purpose demands greater or less completeness. In the *Theaetetus,* where his object is primarily to argue that the categories are not products of sense-perception, but are perceived 'directly by the soul herself without the aid of bodily instruments,' *i.e.* are, as we should say, purely intellectual à priori *forms* of relation, in accord with which mind organises the material of its experience, we find him including in the list being, sameness, difference, likeness, unlikeness, beauty, ugliness, goodness, badness, number. All these, just because they can be predicated of subjects of all kinds, he contends, cannot be cognised by the activity of any special sense. The same dialogue provides us, among other contributions to logical theory, with the important distinction between two kinds of 'change' (*κίνησις*), local motion, or change of position (*φορά*), and alteration, or change of quality (*ἀλλοίωσις*), and with a searching and acute inquiry into the nature of definition, and the conditions under which definition is possible. Among its contributions to terminology we note the new words 'quality' (*ποιότης*=what-likeness), 'organ,' in the sense of a bodily instrument of perception, 'criterion,' 'difference,' in the specifically logical sense afterwards to be made classic by Aristotle. In the *Sophistes*, where the particular distinction between that which the soul perceives through the body, and that which she perceives 'by herself' is in abeyance, the list of 'chief kinds' or classes is given in a briefer form as being, sameness, difference, rest (or changelessness), motion (or change, *κίνησις*). And that dialogue and its continuation the *Politicus* are notable for the prominence given in them, as well as in the introduction to the *Philebus*, to the process of exhaustive logical division of a class into sub-classes by successive acts of dichotomy as a means towards exact definition. Still more interesting, as a contribution to the theory of knowledge, is the main problem with which both the *Theaetetus* and *Sophistes* are really concerned.

Formally the *Theaetetus* deals with the question 'What is knowledge?' and aims at showing that knowledge can neither be identified with sense-perception, as, according to Plato, had been held by Protagoras, nor more generally with 'true belief'; the *Sophistes* professes to be an attempt to illustrate the process of logical definition by finding a satisfactory definition of the class 'sophists.' The actual 'knot' of both dialogues is, however, provided by a paradox of Plato's fellow-Socratic, Antisthenes the Cynic, who had maintained that no term can be truly predicated of any other, *i.e.* that the only true propositions are identities. Plato had already touched upon this paradox in earlier dialogues, the *Euthydemus* and *Cratylus*, where, however, he treats it as a mere extravagance and a fit subject for banter and parody. In the 'dialectical' dialogues he shows himself aware of its real significance for the whole theory of knowledge. Perceiving that the very possibility of science depends upon the possibility of making true propositions in which the subject and predicate are not identical, he sets himself to work to furnish a serious refutation of the doctrine of Antisthenes. An immediate consequence of that doctrine is that genuine error, or 'false opinion,' is impossible.

You cannot think 'what is not' (*i.e.* of any given subject *A* you can only think '*A* is *A*'; you cannot think '*A* is *B*' or '*A* is *C*' if all predication is strictly identical). Hence the problem as to the nature of error becomes fundamental for the inquiry of the *Theaetetus*. In suggesting that knowledge is the same thing as true belief, it is implied that there may be false beliefs, but this is exactly what the doctrine of Antisthenes denied. So in trying to define the 'sophist,' we find ourselves obliged to speak of him as a man who inculcates false beliefs for purposes of gain; but what if the sophist should protest that there is no such thing as a false belief? In the *Theaetetus* the question how error is possible is left unsolved, with the consequence that the dialogue reaches no positive conclusion. We are found, in fact, to have been committing an illogicality in discussing the nature of false belief before arriving at any insight into the nature of truth. One important result is, however, obtained. It is elaborately shown that error may occur not only in judgments which involve a reference to facts of sense-experience, but in those in which both terms belong to the class which the soul 'perceives by herself,' as *e.g.* if a man should mistakenly believe the proposition '$5+7=11$.'

We are thus prepared for the purely logical inquiry into the nature of error which meets us in the *Sophistes.* Plato there finally solves the puzzle by calling attention to the distinction between absolute and relative denial. The 'sophistic' view that to think what is false is impossible had arisen from the argument that thinking what is false means thinking 'what is not,' but to think 'what is not' is impossible, since mere non-entity cannot even be the object of any thought. Plato's reply is that when I think '*A* is not *B*,' I do not mean to assert that *A* is nothing at all, but merely that it is something other than *B*; 'what is not,' in the sense in which a denial can be said to involve thinking of 'what is not,' is simply that which is 'different from' something else, and hence significant denials, both true and false, can be made about any subject. In Platonic language, the 'chief kinds,' or categories, 'have communion' with one another, or can be predicated of one another, and thus significant non-identical predication, as demanded by science, is logically unobjectionable. The familiarity of this result does not in the least detract from its importance in the history of thought, as we may see by reflecting that the fundamental problem of Kant's chief work is the same as Plato's, viz. to justify the universal 'synthetic' propositions of pure science.

In the account given by Aristotle in his *Metaphysics* of Plato's doctrine of 'Ideas,' we are told much that is not explicitly laid down anywhere in the dialogues, and suspicion has accordingly been cast upon the trustworthiness of Aristotle's representations. Such suspicion, however, seems to be excluded when we remember that Aristotle's old fellow-pupil Xenocrates was expounding Platonism at Athens during the whole period of Aristotle's activity as a teacher, and that polemical misrepresentation of Plato's views would, in such circumstances, have been suicidal. According to Aristotle, who appears to be basing his statements upon Plato's more advanced oral teaching, the doctrine of 'Ideas' was presented in a quasi-mathematical form, the 'Ideas' being actually spoken of as 'numbers,' though Plato was careful to distinguish these numbers from the ordinary integers which we use in counting. Each idea was further held to be composed of two factors, the 'One,' which was also identified with the 'Good,' and an element of indetermination and plurality called the 'Indeterminate Duality,' or the 'Great-and-Small.' In virtue of the 'participation' of sensible things in the 'Ideas,' these two elements, the One and the Great-and-Small, are thus ultimately the constituents of the universe. Aristotle adds that Plato regarded the objects of the ordinary mathematical studies as forming a class 'intermediate' between the supreme 'Ideas' or 'Numbers' and physical things. They resemble physical things in so far as there are many of them (many different squares, or circles, and so forth), whereas there is only one 'Idea' of each kind; they resemble the 'Ideas,' and differ from physical things, in being eternally immutable. Thus it would seem that, in the last resort, the concepts or definables of science all presuppose two primarily indefinable notions, that of Unity (which must be carefully distinguished, by the way, from the notion of the integer 1), and that of Multitude (which, again, must not be confused with the notion of cardinal number). Every definable concept can be exhibited as arising by a special mode of combination of these two components. (To illustrate crudely what is plainly meant, consider the character of an ordinary definition. Suppose, *e.g.*, we have *man* defined as a rational mortal being. The class so defined is, on the one hand, one term, or object of thought, the determinate aggregate corresponding to a specific class-concept; on the other, it is equated by the definition with the common part of a plurality (in this case two) of other aggregates. The defined class is thus at once one and many, or rather, a perfectly specific combination of the one and the many.) Since the objects of definition are thus always combinations of the one and the many, we readily see why Plato should have called them 'numbers,' and since the 'one' and 'many' of which they are combinations are not 'the whole number **1**' and 'the series of whole numbers,' but the simpler and prior logical concepts of '*a* term' and '*terms*' (in the plural), we also see why he distinguished these primary 'ideal' numbers from the members of the series of ordinary integers. The whole doctrine, in fact, ceases to be the puzzle that Aristotle found it, when we bring to the study of it some acquaintance with the modern philosophy of number, as expounded by writers like Peano, Frege, and Russell, and bear in mind that something like the reduction of pure mathematics to exact logic effected by these writers was avowedly the goal at which Plato was aiming in his 'dialectic.'

The nearest approximation to the conceptions ascribed to Plato by Aristotle which can be traced in the dialogues must be sought in the

Timaeus and, as has been specially shown by Dr. Henry Jackson, in the *Philebus*. In the *Timaeus* what specially concerns us is the description of the formation of the 'soul of the universe,' and, at a later stage, of the souls of human beings, out of a combination of two ultimate elements, the 'Same,' which symbolises the eternally self-identical, and the 'Other,' which stands for indeterminate mutability and variability. A still closer correspondence is presented by the *Philebus*, in which 'all things that are' are summed up under four categories: (1) the indeterminate, *i.e.* everything that is capable of indefinite variation in number, degree, quantity; (2) the 'limit,' *i.e.* quantitative and numerical determination; (3) the 'mixture of the two,' *i.e.* precisely determined magnitudes and quantities, such as a melody, or an organism; (4) the 'cause of the mixture,' which appears, in the *Philebus*, to be identified with purposive intelligence. Into the discussion of the difficulties which have been raised as to the significance of this classification it is impossible to enter in a work like the present. But it should be noted that, to judge from the examples given of the four 'classes,' Plato is thinking in the *Philebus*, as in the passage of the *Timaeus* just referred to, of the world of everyday 'things' rather than of that of pure concepts. Hence it is probably a mistake to identify any of the four 'classes' with the 'One' and the 'Indeterminate Duality,' or to ask in which class we are to look for the 'Ideas.' We should rather expect to find in his classes factors which are analogous to, but not identical with, those of which the 'Ideas' are composed, and which hold towards 'sensible things' the same relation as that held by the components of the 'Ideas' to the system of scientific concepts. And, in fact, if we identify the 'mixture' with the measured magnitudes of the sensible world, the 'indeterminate' and the 'limit' will be found to occupy towards those magnitudes exactly the position ascribed by Aristotle to the 'One' and the 'Duality' in reference to the 'Ideas.' So again, in the *Timaeus*, while the 'Same' and 'Other' in the composition of the soul are not to be identified with the 'One' and the 'Duality,' they have clearly the same functions; they are to that particular 'mixture' which results from them what 'the One' and 'the Duality' are to the pure logical concept.

To sum up, then, Plato's doctrine of 'Ideas' seems to culminate in the thought that the whole existing universe forms a system exhibiting that character of precise and determinate order and law of which we find the ideal type in the interconnected concepts of a perfected deductive science. When he says that sensible things are 'copies' of the Ideas which are the true objects of science, what he means is that they exhibit everywhere what we now speak of as 'conformity to law.' But for Plato, we must remember, the conformity is never complete in the sensible world; there is an element in all actual sensible experience which defies precise measurement and calculation. Absolute and exact 'conformity to law' is to be found only in the ideal constructions of a pure conceptual science. Or, in other words, so far as such uniformity is actually 'verifiable' in 'experience,' it is only approximate; so far as it is exact and complete, it is always a 'transcendent' ideal. And here, again, his conclusion does not seem to be very different from that of the profoundest modern reflection upon science and her methods.

CHAPTER III

THE SOUL OF MAN—PSYCHOLOGY, ETHICS, AND POLITICS

To understand Plato's scheme of moral and political philosophy, it is necessary first of all to be acquainted with his general conception of the nature of the soul. And this conception is, again, best approached by starting from the simple ethics and psychology of Socrates. The ethical and psychological doctrine of Socrates, as we can reconstruct it by comparison of the works of Plato and Xenophon and the notices which have come down to us of the views of the other 'Socratic men,' may be summed up in the one proposition that 'virtue is knowledge.' Primarily this proposition may be said to be a psychological one. It means that the one and only function of mental life is cognition; the mind is just a 'knowing and perceiving subject,' and nothing more. From this it follows at once that there is one, and only one, 'virtue' or 'excellence' possible to mind, the adequate performance of its characteristic function of knowing, and one and only one defect or 'vice,' or mal-performance of function, viz. intellectual error. Hence we can immediately deduce all the familiar paradoxes of the Socratic morality; that all the 'virtues' are really one, that all wrongdoing is simply error of judgment, that no man can know what is good for him without doing it, and that wrong action is consequently always involuntary. The ethical advances made by Plato upon Socrates and those Socratics who, like Antisthenes the Cynic, clung to the simple psychology of the master, are all connected with the discovery that mental life is in reality a much more complex thing than Socrates had supposed.

It is interesting to trace the way in which Plato is gradually led to replace the Socratic conception of the soul by a view which is more complex and does more justice to the facts of moral experience. The earliest group of the dialogues are, as we have seen, in the main concerned with the peculiarly Socratic problem of arriving at definitions of the commonly received moral 'virtues.' The course of the investigation, in most cases, proceeds as follows. It is proposed to determine the exact meaning of some currently used name of a virtue or moral excellence, such as 'self-control (in the *Charmides*) or 'courage' (in the *Laches*). Usually the respondent of the dialogue begins by falling into the mistake of propounding an enumeration of different instances of the virtue in question. Then, upon his attention being called by Socrates to the difference between the enumeration of the members of a class and the definition of the class-concept, he proceeds to propound one or more definitions of a loose and popular kind. These definitions are tested by comparison with some example of the virtue in question to which they will manifestly not apply, and thus shown to be insufficient, as *e.g.* in Book I. of the *Republic*, where the tentative definitions of 'justice' as 'paying what one owes,' or 'doing good to one's friends and harm to one's enemies,' are shown to be defective by the reflections that there are cases in which it would not be unjust to withhold repayment of a deposit, and that a virtuous man as such will never willingly do harm to any one. In the purely Socratic type of dialogue, Socrates usually next leads up to a definition in which the virtue under examination is identified with some form of knowledge, as when 'self-control' or 'temperance' is identified in the *Charmides* with self-knowledge, or true courage, in the *Laches*, with knowledge of what is and what is not formidable. On closer examination, however, it is found that we are unable to say what particular form of knowledge corresponds to the particular virtue in question, so that the identification of virtue with knowledge leads to an inability to distinguish any one special moral excellence from virtue in general. (Thus in the *Laches*, when courage has been defined as 'knowledge of what is and is not formidable,' it is pointed out that a formidable thing simply means a future or impending evil, so that the definition really amounts to the statement that courage is 'knowledge of what is and what is not really evil,' and hence fails to apply to courage in particular as distinguished from other morally excellent qualities.) The formal result in such dialogues is thus the merely negative one that we have learned our own ignorance about matters of the gravest import with which we believed ourselves to be perfectly acquainted, but it is easy to read between the lines that the true source of the difficulty has been the one-sided Socratic reduction of all mental activity to cognition. It is this over-simplification of the psychological facts which has made it impossible to distinguish one form of moral excellence from another.

Nowhere is the defect of the Socratic moral psychology more clearly brought out than in the *Protagoras*, the literary masterpiece of Plato's earliest period. Here the original question propounded is whether moral virtue can be taught by a master to a pupil, as of course should be possible if virtue is simply a form of knowledge. Protagoras is, as becomes a professional teacher of morals, quite sure that it can; Socrates feels a doubt, due to the facts that persons who are most careful about the education of their children make no attempt to provide them with expert instruction in 'virtue,' as in other accomplishments, and that the public assembly, which in general refuses to take the advice of a layman against that of a specialist in any branch of knowledge, regards the opinion of any one citizen as to the morality of a proposed course of action as being equally valuable with that of any other. In the course of the discussion which follows, the original question is, by an apparent irrelevance, replaced by the problem whether virtue is one or many, Protagoras strongly advocating the popular view that there are a variety of entirely distinct types of virtue, and that the same man may possess one of them, *e.g.* justice, in a high degree, and yet be sadly deficient in another, *e.g.* courage; Socrates, for his part, champions the doctrine that there is only one kind of virtue, which is knowledge, by expounding the now familiar doctrine of egoistic Hedonism. Virtue is the right estimation of the pleasurable and painful consequences of our actions; vice is always miscalculation, and arises from miscomputation of the relative amounts of pleasure and pain to which a given act will lead. Thus, as Plato is careful to point out, at the end of the discussion the two parties have changed places. Protagoras, who had been sure that virtue can be taught like any science or art, is equally sure that it is a paradox to identify it with knowledge; Socrates, who was inclined to deny its teachability, is found to be maintaining that it is knowledge and nothing else. The apparently lame conclusion of the dialogue has caused much embarrassment to interpreters who have failed to sympathise with Plato's dramatic irony. But the real point which Plato is anxious to make is clear. If Protagoras, by treating each moral excellence as altogether different in kind from every other, has made it impossible to frame any single conception of 'virtue' as a whole, Socrates, by treating virtue as simply identical with knowledge, has equally failed to make any discrimination possible between the different 'virtues.'

We are taken a step further towards a more adequate moral psychology in the dialogue *Meno.* Here, again, we are met by the old question how virtue can be the same thing as knowledge, if there is avowedly no such thing as a recognised science of good action with a body of professional teachers of its principles. The answer is suggested that possibly virtue depends not upon scientific knowledge but on 'correct opinion.' In that case, we need not be surprised that what virtue we find in the world is not the result of professional scientific instruction, since, though knowledge can only be obtained by proof, 'correct opinions' about a subject may be held by persons who have no insight into the reasoned grounds for their opinions, and are thus not possessed of real knowledge. If the discussion in the *Meno* were not arbitrarily cut short at the point where this suggestion has been reached, it would, of course, have been necessary to proceed to the question, in what way a 'correct opinion,' which is not knowledge, about the morally good and bad can be produced in the soul. The full answer to this question is given by the theory of education worked out in the *Republic,* and that theory, in its turn, depends on the psychological distinction between the 'parts' of the soul, which is expounded most fully in the *Republic* and *Timaeus*, and mythically set forth in the imposing allegory of the *Phaedrus*. Plato's great psychological discovery may be briefly condensed into the phrase that the soul is neither a mere undifferentiated unit, nor a mere plurality of independent and disconnected activities, but both a One and a Many. It is, indeed, a unity, and not, as the *Theaetetus* puts it, a sort of 'Trojan horse,' or congeries of distinct activities, but it is a unity within which we can distinguish a plurality of different functions, or, as Plato more naïvely calls them, 'parts' or 'kinds.' Of such 'parts' or 'kinds' there are three: a part with which we reason, the calculative or rational part; a part with which we feel the appetitive cravings connected with the satisfaction of our organic bodily needs, the 'appetitive part'; a part made up of the higher and nobler emotions, chief among which Plato reckons the emotions of righteous indignation and scorn of what is base; hence the general name for this element is with him, the 'spirited' part. Later Platonism of a popular kind was frequently content to group the second and third 'parts' together, in opposition to the rational element, under the common name of the 'irrational' part of the soul, a simplification for which Plato himself prepares the way in the *Timaeus.* The existence of these distinct elements in mental life is primarily proved in the *Republic* by appeal to the facts of individual psychology. Our common experience of the conflict between rational judgment as to what is good and appetite is, taken in conjunction with the law of Contradiction, sufficient to establish the distinction between the 'part of the soul which reasons or reflects' and 'the part wherewith we crave.' The further recognition of the 'spirited' element is then based upon the consideration that the higher emotions may be enlisted on the side of reason in its struggle with appetite, as we see, *e.g.*, from the sense of indignation with ourselves which arises when we have stooped to the gratification of an appetite which reason condemns. The distinction thus obtained is then confirmed by appeal to our experience of the broad differences in character between races and social classes. Thus the Greeks, as a people, are pre-eminent in and devoted to science; the northern barbarians are distinguished by their unreflecting impetuous daring; the Phœnicians and Egyptians by skill in and devotion to commerce—the organised ministering to the appetites. So again, in any society, there are three main distinguishable classes: the devotees of knowledge, of prowess, of merchandise; or, again, the wise counsellors, the daring soldiers, the industrial class. Now, whence do these differences in racial and class character spring, if not from a corresponding difference in the mental constitution of individuals, according as one or other of the three 'kinds' is predominant? The result thus obtained becomes, as we shall see, of fundamental importance not only for Plato's theory of education, but for his classification and estimate of the different forms of political and social organisation, and for his Philosophy of History. It may, in fact, be said to be the connecting thread by which the vast range of inquiries taken up in the *Republic* are held together in an artistic unity. In the *Timaeus* the same psychological distinction reappears in a more accentuated form as the basis of what we might call a simple Psycho-physics. The three 'parts' are there described as three distinct 'souls': one, the 'rational' soul, being immortal and having its seat in the brain; the other two, 'spirit' and 'appetite,' being mortal, and located in the thorax and abdomen respectively. In the *Phaedrus* we find the same ideas symbolically expressed by the representation of the soul as a human charioteer (reason) borne by a pair of horses, the one nobler (spirit), the other baser (appetite).

It will be noticed that Plato's psychological analysis thus corresponds to none of those with which modern psychology has made us familiar. Neither 'conation' nor 'feeling,' in our modern sense, receives a distinct place in the scheme. Both are, in fact, regarded as features of each of the three 'parts of the soul.' As Plato himself puts it, in the *Republic,* for each 'part' there is a corresponding 'life,' with characteristic 'desires,' 'pleasures,' and 'pains' of its own. In particular, 'will' must, of course, in Plato's scheme, be identified with intelligent choice, and thus be assigned to the reasoning faculty or function. Hence it has been correctly said that Plato's 'parts of the soul' represent rather three different levels of mental development than three different 'aspects' or 'features' of the individual psychical process.

Before we proceed to examine the ethical and political scheme based by Plato upon this analysis of the human mind, it is desirable to say something in general about his conception of the destiny and dignity of the soul. As is well known, Plato repeatedly insists both upon the immortality and the pre-existence of the individual soul. There is, indeed, a difficulty as to whether it is to the whole tripartite soul or only to its rational part that he means to ascribe these characteristics. The source of the difficulty is partly to be found in the fact that Plato's language on these matters is almost always tinged with a greater or smaller admixture of imaginative myth, partly perhaps in a modification of his views with advancing age. In the *Phaedo* and *Meno* we hear merely of the pre-existence and deathlessness of the 'soul' without further qualification. In the *Republic* a formal proof is offered for the immortality of the 'soul,' but a hint is dropped by the way that our tripartite analysis of the soul may only hold good of it in its incarnate state, and that the question whether it is ultimately one or many might receive a different answer if we could contemplate it apart from the effects of its connection with the body. In the *Timaeus*, as we have already said, the 'rational' soul is explicitly distinguished as immortal from its mortal concomitants, which are represented as being added expressly to adapt it to its conjunction with a mortal body.

Plato's arguments for immortality and pre-existence are set forth principally in the *Meno*,

Phaedo, Republic, and *Timaeus.* The best-known of the arguments for immortality are those of the *Phaedo,* which may be summarised as follows: (1) On the analogy of our experience of various rhythmical processes, such as those of expansion and contraction, sleeping and waking, it is urged that the processes of the universe in general are cyclical, or, as Plato puts it, that 'opposites' arise from and give birth to each other. In the case of the 'opposites' death and life, we see in experience only one half of the cycle, the process of dying, by which life gives place to death; but on grounds of analogy it is reasonable to postulate the existence of a corresponding reverse process by which the dead return again to life. In fact, unless there exists such a reverse process, the ultimate fate of the universe must be the entire cessation of life. The argument thus, like many of the deductions of Herbert Spencer, turns on the assumption that all processes in nature are marked by cyclical rhythm, and from our point of view is exposed to the objection that the alleged reversibility of all natural processes is in conflict with the second law of Thermo-dynamics. A modern physicist might, in fact, declare that the ultimate extinction of life, treated by Plato as an absurdity, is precisely the doom which, in virtue of the dissipation of energy, he anticipates for the universe. (2) A second analogy on which Plato lays stress is that between the soul which knows and the objects of true knowledge. Like the concepts which science contemplates, the soul is invisible, immaterial, incapable of dissipation into locally separate constituents; whereas the body is visible, material, composed of separable ingredients. It is natural then to infer, that while the body is, like the rest of the changing physical world, perishable, the soul is so far akin to the eternal as to be imperishable. (3) More definite consequences are drawn from the famous Platonic doctrine, to be explained immediately, according to which scientific knowledge is really a process of 'recollection' of truths with which the mind was already familiar in a previous state of existence. This doctrine, if accepted, proves pre-existence, and thus establishes at least the possibility of continued existence of the disembodied soul after death. (4) The crowning argument of the *Phaedo* is an ontological one. The 'soul' is itself the very principle of life, and produces life everywhere where it is present. Life is thus what would be called in the later technical language of Aristotle an *essential* attribute of soul. Consequently death, the 'opposite' of life, can never be truly predicated of that which is the principle of life itself. A 'dead soul' would be a contradiction in terms. The soul, therefore, is deathless, and it is an easy inference that what can survive death is absolutely indestructible.

The flaw in this ontological argument is fairly patent. We may readily rejoin that, in proving that there is no such thing as a dead soul, we have by no means proved that the soul still exists or is anything at all after the death of the body. It is therefore not surprising that the *Republic*, while alluding in passing to the 'other' arguments for immortality, should present a new argument of a moral kind intended to make the indestructibility of soul more certain. This argument runs as follows. Nothing that is can be destroyed except by its own proper and specific 'evil.' Thus, *e.g.*, the human body can only perish from diseases, etc., specific to the animal organism; other causes, such as the unwholesomeness of our food, can only bring about death indirectly by first leading to some specific disease of our organism. Now the specific 'evil' of the soul is wickedness, and consequently, if the soul is destructible at all, the immediate cause of its destruction must always be this specific 'evil'; if it dies of anything, it must die of wickedness.

But experience shows that wickedness is far from diminishing the soul's vitality; on the contrary, it often appears, when conjoined with great mental capacity, to intensify it. (Plato is, of course, thinking of that conjunction of mental energy with moral perversity which we are accustomed to associate with such names as those of the Borgias or of Napoleon.) If the specific 'evil' of the soul is thus incapable of destroying it, we may safely infer that it is secure against all dissolution. In the *Phaedrus* the argument for immortality, as previously presented by the *Phaedo*, is condensed into the general contention that 'soul' is the source of all movement and process in the universe. All movement whatever is either self-originated or received by communication from without. And, to escape from an endless regress, we are obliged to hold that movement initiated from without has always its ultimate source in a prior self-originated or spontaneous movement. Now that which has the power of spontaneous movement is soul. Hence, if soul could cease to be, all movement would ultimately disappear from the universe. And since this universal cessation of movement is, as we have seen, unthinkable for Plato, he infers that soul, the ultimate source of movement, is imperishable.

The argument for pre-existence is put before us in the *Meno*, and apparently with a direct reference to that dialogue, again in the *Phaedo*. The premise upon which it is based is the epistemological doctrine that scientific knowledge is recollection of what we have previously known. This conviction itself is derived from Plato's conception of the 'transcendent' character of purely scientific, that is to say, mathematical truth. Since sense-experience never presents more than an imperfect approximation to the relations cognised in scientific knowledge, it follows that the source of such knowledge is not sense-experience. Sense-experience, at best, only serves to recall to the mind by suggestion ideal concepts derived from a non-empirical source. In the *Meno* Socrates illustrates this position by putting appropriate questions to an uneducated slave, and thus eliciting from him a correct perception of mathematical truths in which he has never been instructed. Scientific truth is thus shown to be of a non-empirical *à priori* character, and the interpretation given by Plato to this fact is that what we commonly call the 'learning' of a science is simply a process in which the soul 'recollects' truths of which she was already in unconscious possession. She must then, it is argued, have been in existence, and have been acquainted with these pure *à priori* truths, before her incarnation in the body. It is this same conviction of the non-empirical character of scientific truth which leads Plato to describe the process of education in the *Republic* in opposition to views which place the essence of education in the communication of information from without, as a 'turning round of the eye of the soul to behold the light,' and in the *Theaetetus* to liken the function of the philosophic teacher to that of the midwife.

In the great myths of the *Gorgias, Republic, Phaedo, Phaedrus*, and the half-mythical cosmogony of the *Timaeus*, these convictions as to immortality and pre-existence are made the basis for an imaginative picture of the fortunes and destiny of the soul, in which the details are borrowed partly from Pythagorean astronomy, partly from the Pythagorean and Orphic religious mythology, the main purpose of the whole being to impress the imagination with a sense of the eternal significance of right moral choice. The as yet unembodied soul is pictured in the *Phaedrus* under the figure of a charioteer borne on a car drawn by two winged steeds (spirit and appetite), in the train of the great procession of the gods, whose goal, as they move round the vault of heaven, is that 'place above the heavens' where the eternal bodiless Ideas may be contemplated in all their purity. The soul which fails to control its coursers sinks to earth, 'loses its wings,' and becomes incarnate in a mortal body, forgetting the 'imperial palace whence it came.' Its recollections may, however, be awakened by the influence of beauty, the only 'Idea' which is capable of presentation through the medium of the senses. Love of beauty rightly cultivated develops into love of wisdom and of all high and sacred things; the 'wings' of the soul thus begin to sprout once more. After one earthly life is over, there follows a period of retribution for the good and evil deeds done in the body, and, when that is ended, the choice of a second bodily life. The soul which has thrice in succession chosen the worthiest life, that of the lover of wisdom, is thereafter dismissed to live unencumbered by the body in spiritual converse with heavenly things. For others, a pilgrimage of ten thousand years, composed of ten bodily lives with the period of one thousand year's retribution after each life, is necessary before the soul can become fully 'winged' and return to her first station in the heavens. In the *Republic* Plato professes to describe by the mouth of a witness brought back from the world of the dead what happens at one of the times of incarnation succeeding upon the close of a period of retribution. The assembled souls, some returning from rewards in heaven for the good deeds of their last incarnate life, others ascending from a purgatorial prison-house of the evil (both here and in the *Phaedo* Plato provides for the unending punishment only of one or two hopelessly bad malefactors on a colossal scale), are mustered before the thrones of the Fates and bidden to choose, each for himself, a life from a number of lives which are placed before them. For each 'life' it is set down what its outward destinies and circumstances are to be, but not what degree of virtue is to accompany it. For virtue depends not on fate, but on the character of the soul, and a man shall have more or less of it according as he honours it or contemns it. The choice of a new 'life' is left free to the individual soul; 'the responsibility is with the chooser, God is clear thereof'—words which in a later age were adopted as a battle-cry by the partisans of human freedom against the Stoic predestinationism. According to the tastes and dispositions of the individual souls, and to the degree of wisdom they have derived from philosophy or from experience, they make their choice, and this, once made, is irrevocable. In this process a soul which has inhabited a human body may come to be incarnate in that of some animal of qualities akin to itself, or, *vice versa*, a soul which dwelt last in an animal body may become that of a human being at its next birth.

The Orphic fancy of transmigration meets us again not only in the *Phaedo*, but also in the less highly mythical *Timaeus*, where the more crude pictures of hell and purgatory have been discarded. In the *Timaeus* the souls of those who are hereafter to be born as men are fashioned by God at the first making of the world, and each is assigned to its special star, where it may learn those laws of the universal order of things in obedience to which our happiness stands. At the appointed time the various souls are cast, like seeds, into the bosom of Earth and of the planets, and are brought forth thence as men literally 'sprung from the soil.' After death, those who have lived best in the body are reincarnated as men, those who have lived worse as women, or as inferior animals of different kinds according to the degree of their shortcomings. Thus Plato offers us a curious kind of evolutionary theory *à rebours*.

It is not easy to decide how far any details of these myths are to be taken as seriously meant. According to Plato himself, the myth is, strictly speaking, a falsehood or 'fiction,' and its value lies simply in the moral effect of the emotions it arouses upon character. Judged from this point of view, Plato's own stories of the fortunes of the soul are to be estimated primarily as an imaginative expression of a deep conviction of the supreme importance of right conduct and good living; incidentally, also, they enable him to indicate his opinions on the astronomical structure of the world, and to show by an example what might be made of the popular mythology if it were overhauled and remodelled with a view to enlisting it on the side of a sound morality. For the Platonic *philosophy* the myths can hardly be said to have any direct significance. For, in Plato's opinion, knowledge is entirely concerned with the transcendent concepts of pure deductive science; all that we commonly call the world of experience and 'actual fact' belongs for him to the realm of 'becoming,' *i.e.* of largely incalculable change and variation, as opposed to that of unchanging 'being,' and for this reason falls outside the scope of science rightly so-called. Hence, when he would speak of these matters at all, he can only do so by means of a 'likely story,' which makes no claim to set forth scientific truth. The notion, common since the days of Neo-Platonism, that the myth is the appropriate form in which to symbolise truths too sublime for rational comprehension, is entirely foreign to Plato. It is precisely when he is dealing with what he regards as the ultimate realities that his language is most 'scientific' and least mythical.

To return to the subject of the Platonic theory of ethics and politics. We can now see how Plato's more developed psychology enables him to escape the most obvious difficulties created by the Socratic identification of virtue with intellectual insight. Since the soul itself contains a non-rational as well as a rational factor, complete moral excellence must consist in the maintenance of the proper relation between the two, and the attainment of the proper development of each. But the proper relation between the two is that the higher and worthier element should rule and the inferior obey, just as the right relation between classes, upon which the salvation of a community depends, is that the worthier and fitter should govern and the inferior obey. It is only in this relation that the inferior itself 'makes the most' of its powers and enjoys the highest good possible to it. The moral ideal is thus a condition in which the passions and emotions are developed in accord with a supreme law of life dictated by rational insight. Hence Plato finds himself in opposition at once to the one-sided intellectualism of the Cynics, the most faithful continuers of the Socratic tradition which identifies virtue with mere intellectual insight, and to the fashionable Hedonism which regards the gratification of desires as they arise, no matter what their character, as the chief good of man. Against the Cynic he urges that the definition of the good as 'insight' is circular, since, when pressed to say what is the object of such insight, you are driven to reply that it is insight into 'the good'; and further, that none of us would seriously choose as the best life one of purely intellectual insight unaccompanied by any form of gratified feeling. Against the Hedonist whose ideal is a life of varied and intense desires and passions, with complete satisfaction for them all, Plato contends that such an ideal is essentially self-contradictory. To say nothing of the vulgarity and unworthiness of some very intense satisfactions, the intensity of satisfaction depends very largely upon the intensity of the preceding sense of want and dissatisfaction, and is, therefore, to a great extent, illusory. A principal ingredient, for instance, in our most intense experiences of bodily pleasure, is the sense of relief from preceding bodily distress. (Compare Shelley's well-known line about the 'unrest which men miscall delight.') And, since our appetites grow by what they feed on, to live for the Hedonist's end means to cultivate passions which are constantly becoming more and more imperative, while their gratifications are at the same time becoming less and less satisfactory. Hence the life of the 'tyrant,' who by his position is better enabled than any other man to gratify his passions without scruple, so far from being the happiest, is really the most wretched of existences. Just because he always 'does what he pleases,' he never succeeds in doing what he really wishes.

In the *Republic*, and more fully in the *Philebus*, Plato works out this line of thought into a distinction between two kinds of pleasure, the 'pure' and the 'mixed.' Pure pleasures are those which do not depend on a previous painful sense of want, and are thus not mingled with the element of mere relief from pain. They are *wholly* pleasurable, and there is no element of illusion about the experience of them. Prominent among them are, of purely physical pleasures, those of the sense of smell; of others, the æsthetic pleasures derived from the contemplation of beauty of form, colour, and tone, and the pleasures which attend the acquisition of knowledge. The pleasures of appetite are 'impure' or 'mixed'; they derive most of their intensity from the contrast with the previous painful tension of unsatisfied appetite, and their apparent delightfulness is thus chiefly an illusion. Hence for the man who desires true happiness a small quantity of 'pure' pleasure is more valuable than a very large amount of 'mixed' pleasure; in other words, pleasures are to be estimated by their quality rather than by their quantity. On this ground Plato maintains that even from the point of view of pleasurableness itself, the life of the 'lover of wisdom,' because richer in 'pure' and undeceptive pleasure, is preferable to that of the man who lives for the satisfaction of ambition or appetite.

Plato's psychology further makes it possible for him to do justice to the consideration that a certain degree of moral virtue may be attained by the man who has merely 'correct opinions' without philosophic insight. In the last resort, indeed, insight and virtue cannot be separated, since the 'excellence' of a soul means its adequate realisation of its functions and capabilities, and this is only possible in a life in which the action of the irrational elements is prescribed by rational insight into the 'good,' *i.e.* into the place of human nature in the scheme of things. But one who possesses this insight himself may employ it to provide training and discipline for the emotions and appetites of others who do not themselves possess it, and to whom morality comes, therefore, as a body of 'right opinions' as to what is good or bad, accepted on authority apart from personal insight into the grounds for them. Hence, in the *Republic*, Plato is able to recognise a higher and a lower stage of moral excellence. The lower stage is what he calls the virtue of a 'citizen,' the moral state of a loyal member of a well-governed community, whose emotions and appetites have been disciplined in accord with the laws of right living as laid down by wise rulers, themselves acquainted by philosophy with the true nature of society and the human soul, and the rational ends of action. The higher is constituted by the virtue of the genuine philosopher, in whom obedience to the laws of right living rests upon personal insight into the 'good.' The inferior level of excellence is demanded of all citizens of Plato's ideal community, and is to be produced in them by a moral education, begun in their earliest years, which aims at the formation of character by discipline of the passions and emotions; the superior is to be attained only by the chosen few as the final outcome of an intellectual training which supervenes on the preliminary discipline of the irrational nature, proceeds in order through the whole sphere of science, and culminates in the 'dialectic' which reveals the true character of 'good.' Thus Plato's scheme of moral education anticipates the Aristotelian distinction between 'virtues of character' (*ἠθικαὶ ἀρεταί*) and 'excellences of intellect,' and more distantly the seductive but dangerous ecclesiastical conception of a distinction between the virtues which suffice for the ordinary life of humanity, and the higher qualifications of the select few who aspire to 'perfection.'

In this scheme Socraticism has preserved its essential spirit by the sacrifice of its letter Virtue is no longer a mere unity, since each factor in the soul has its own specific 'excellence,' precisely because it has its own characteristic function to discharge. Yet insight retains its primacy for the practical life, inasmuch as it is the philosopher's insight into the true nature of man and the true end of life which prescribes the lines along which the subordinate 'parts' of the soul are to be allowed to develop. The consequence is that with Plato the leading types of virtue, the quadrilateral of the since familiar 'cardinal' virtues, form a plurality of excellences corresponding to the plurality of functions in the soul, but a plurality which is made into a harmonious system by the presence of a single guiding principle.

The leading forms of virtue are assumed by Plato to be roughly represented by the names justice, wisdom, courage (literally manliness, *ἀνδρεία*), *sophrosyne*. This last untranslatable term has been variously rendered in English by 'temperance,' 'continence,' 'self-control,' equivalents which are all objectionable from the implication of painful self-restraint which they carry with them. Etymologically, the nearest rendering would perhaps be 'healthy-mindedness,' a word which has unfortunate associations for the American branch at least of the English-speaking community. The uses of the word in Greek literature indicate that the quality for which it stood to Plato's contemporaries was that moral gracefulness, beauty, sense of form and proportion which is the opposite of ὕβρις, 'insolence,' 'absence of moral good taste,' and is inculcated by the traditional precept of Delphi, 'Nothing overmuch.' In fact, our readiest way to understand *sophrosyne* is, I think, to conceive of the inward and ethical counterpart of the temper and manner which we know in its minor outward manifestations as 'good form.' Three of these virtues are identified by Plato with the characteristic excellences of the three 'parts' or functions of the soul. Wisdom is specifically proper discharge of function in the 'part with which we reason'; courage is the right and perfect condition of 'spirit' which has been trained to fear or be ashamed of the things a man ought to fear or to feel shame for, and no others; *sophrosyne* is an ordered and disciplined condition of the appetites. For complete virtue there must be perfect harmony in the execution of function by the various 'parts' of the soul. A man does his work in the world—which is to live—well, only when there is a due and proper subordination between the different elements in his character; when wisdom prescribes the end and rule of life; when the emotions of righteous indignation, chivalry, honour, loyalty, are enlisted in the support of wisdom and its law, and the appetites have been schooled by habit into willing obedience. Justice, then, the virtue which common language recognises as somehow embracing all the rest, when we speak of a 'just' man as equivalent to a 'righteous man,' must consist precisely in the maintenance of this harmony and due subordination between the various functions of the soul. A man will be 'just,' when each 'part' of the soul 'does its own business' and does not usurp functions which belong to another 'part,' *i.e.* when the development of each 'part' is controlled by the maintenance of the proper subordination of lower to higher. In this way Plato in the *Republic* lays down the leading principles of that conception of the moral life which we, rather unjustly, have come to connect in common speech with the name of his disciple Aristotle.

It is the same in the State, or community of citizens, as in the lesser internal 'polity' of man. For the State is simply the individual man writ large. To the distinctions between the 'parts' of the soul correspond the distinctions between the three classes into which a community naturally falls, the statesmen, the soldiers, the artisans and retailers. The first of these classes serves the community by its wisdom, the second by its prowess and trained strength, the third by making provision for the satisfaction of the bodily needs. And the State is a well-ordered and justly governed State when its institutions and laws are framed by the wisdom of the statesman, supported loyally against the enemy from without and sedition from within by the valour of the soldier, loyally accepted and obeyed by the industrial population. Justice, in the community as in the individual, means that each organ is to 'do its own business'; there is to be a proper sub-division of function, each social class contenting itself with efficient performance of its own special part in maintaining the existence of the community, and none usurping a part which it is not fitted to execute. The conception of public duty which we sometimes express by saying that individuals and classes ought to regard their powers and possessions as held in trust for the community has never received a more thoroughgoing exposition than in the social system advocated as ideal in the *Republic* of Plato.

The *Republic* begins as an inquiry into what we should now term an ethical rather than a political question, the question, What is justice? But for Plato, as for Greek thought in general, there is no real distinction between the spheres of ethics and politics. If we would see what justice is, and what is its connection with the admitted end of human action, happiness, or 'living well,' we must not be content to study justice and its workings as they reveal themselves on a small scale in the life of a single individual, who may very possibly be out of tune with the general organisation of his place and time; we must ask ourselves what would human life be like in a community in which institutions, customs, educational traditions, were all expressly organised with a view to the complete embodiment of the principle of justice, and how would such a community compare, in respect of satisfactoriness of life, with the communities known to us from experience and history. Thus the Platonic Socrates, in order to vindicate the position that justice is in itself, apart from any ulterior consequences, a better thing than injustice, and the life of the just man a better life than that of the unjust man, however lucky or successful he may be, finds himself led to consider the characteristics of the ideal State. As is usual with Plato, the starting-point for the great ideal construction is sought in what looks at first like a very simple and prosaic fact of experience. The first requisite of a decently ordered community is found in the economic principle of the division of labour. Utility demands that each man shall have his own special calling, and that his abilities shall not be frittered away by compelling him to do several things indifferently rather than one thing well. It is this economic maxim of 'one man, one trade,' which we subsequently discover to contain the fundamental principle of moral conduct and the basis of a philosophy of education. The first sign of its extended significance is its application to the problem of national defence. War is an inevitable feature of national growth, and for the successful conduct of war it is not enough to rely, as the Greeks of the fifth century had done everywhere except in Sparta, on the amateur valour of the ordinary citizen. We must have an army which consists of citizens who are also professional soldiers, trained mentally and morally, as well as physically, with a view to military efficiency. Thus Plato begins his organisation of society by distinguishing two classes in his community: the ordinary industrial, and the trained defender or 'guardian' of national safety. At a later stage the correspondence between the 'parts' of the soul and the classes of the community is made complete by a further selection from the 'guardians' of a smaller group of specially able persons who are to form the class of statesmen. (It should be noted that Plato has already silently indicated a marked innovation on established custom. It is implied that there is to be no class of slaves in the community. Manufactures, as well as agriculture, the only industrial pursuit generally recognised in Greece as worthy of a freeman, are to be in the hands of the non-military citizens.)

The selection of the 'guardians' is to begin at birth; from the very first, children who exhibit superiority in the characteristics requisite for a 'guardian' are to be set apart and subjected to a systematic educational preparation for their future duties, while care is taken to prevent the degeneration of the scheme into a hard-and-fast system of castes by frequent examinations and tests, and the degrading of the unfit into a lower class, as well as by the promotion of the deserving and capable members of a lower class to a higher. Thus there is to be throughout the State a *carrière ouverte aux talents.* The qualities specially desirable in a 'guardian' will be courage and gentleness, when found in combination, and the object of the educational system will be to preserve a balance between the two by a training which shall harden its recipients against the solicitations of pain and pleasure, while imparting to them a spirit of open-mindedness and love of cultivation. Plato wishes in fact, to combine the strength and hardness of the Spartan character with the flexibility and interest in things of the mind of the Athenian, while avoiding the Spartan's tendency to intellectual narrowness and 'boorishness,' and the Athenian besetting fault of moral levity and instability. His State is to unite in an ideal Greek character all that is best both in Sparta and in Athens, or perhaps we should rather say, in Dorian character and Ionian intellect, just as some modern thinkers have dreamed of a union of 'Hebraic' moral earnestness and 'Hellenic' intellectual cultivation in a single type.

He finds the material for the double moral education he desires in the current Hellenic conception of 'gymnastics' and 'music' (*i.e.* the rudiments of literature, together with the art of singing and accompanying oneself on the lyre), as the two branches of a gentleman's education. But he proposes to reform both these departments. Against the current view that gymnastic provides training for the body, music for the mind, he insists that the ultimate object of both is to train the mind. The object of gymnastic is to make brave and efficient soldiers, not specialised athletes who can make 'records' or perform special feats, but are useless for the general service of the community. Hence the physical training of his 'guardians' is to be throughout adapted to the production of all-round military efficiency of mind and body. In 'music' his reforms are of a more far-reaching character. On the literary side, the 'musical' education of the Athenian gentleman consisted first and foremost in acquaintance with the poems of Homer and Hesiod, the great repositories of accepted religious tradition, and with some of the compositions of the gnomic and lyric poets which were to the Greek what such works as the 'wisdom literature' of the Bible are to ourselves, sources of generally venerated ethical precept. To estimate the amount of an Athenian's literary culture, we must also add an acquaintance with the chief productions of the great national dramatists. But Plato, like many thinkers before him, was more repelled than attracted by the moral tone of the national sacred literature, and accordingly proposes to subject it to drastic revision.

We cannot expect a high standard of conduct in a community which is accustomed to believe immoral stories about the beings whom it worships and reveres. Accordingly Plato lays down two canons to be observed in all tales told to the young about gods or heroes. God, being good, cannot be the author of evil; God cannot lie. On the strength of these two principles, the greater part of the poetical mythology is at once condemned. Further, the great heroes of old must never be represented as indulging in unseemly passions or mercenary calculations of self-interest, nor must the unseen world be painted in the horrific colours of popular ghost-lore, unless we mean to train our pupils to be cowards and afraid of death. But if epic poetry is to be thus thoroughly overhauled, the drama fares even worse. Plato would, in fact, prohibit tragedy and comedy altogether. Partly this sentence is based upon the conviction that an impressionable spectator tends to become assimilated in his own character to that which is enacted before him for his amusement, and hence a large part of the current drama is to be rejected as imitative of things and persons which are merely vulgar and base. Partly, Plato, with his deep-rooted conviction that a man can only play one part on the stage of life efficiently, and that only when his life has been given to the learning of it, dreads the effect of devotion to the drama in making his citizens 'versatile.' He would not have them brilliantly superficial, quick at posing, at echoing ideas or counterfeiting emotions which do not come from the depths of their nature. He has a horror of 'bohemianism' and the 'artistic temperament.' For similar reasons he would expel from education, as tending to excite unwholesome moods of feeling, all the current 'modes' or 'scales' of music, except the Dorian and Phrygian.

The attack upon art is renewed with even more bitterness in the last book of the *Republic*, which goes so far as to demand the absolute suppression of poetry. The poet, we are there told, is a mere caricaturist. He copies vulgar everyday experience, which is itself a mere inaccurate copy of the true 'types' or 'Ideas' of things, and he does not even copy it without distortion. (The underlying thought is thus that coarse and imperfect as are our common everyday notions of human life and character, and our current ideas of conduct, 'literature' is an exaggeration and perversion even of them.) Plato's language shows that his judgment has been largely inspired by hostility to 'realistic' tendencies in the letters and art of his time, but it is an economy of the truth to represent him as intending his censure to fall only upon bad realistic' art. He seriously means, against his own inclinations, to prohibit imaginative literature and art as such,

There is no more pathetic example of the irony of human history than this spectacle of the greatest literary genius of Greece, in his zeal for truth and clearness of vision, proposing to sacrifice all which has made Greece most precious to the world.

The early education thus planned by Plato for his statesmen and soldiers is intended to provide for them up to the age of incipient manhood. It will be noted that it is primarily altogether a discipline for character and taste; the strictly intellectual education supervenes at a later stage, and is, for the most part, confined to the most select class of all, the exceptional few who are judged competent to serve the community as its rulers. Before he enters upon any account of it, Plato has first to explain and defend three paradoxical features by which the organisation of the projected state is to be marked. (1) In the 'guardian classes' there is to be no such thing as private property or a private family. The 'guardians' are to receive from the community at large the means of their support, but are to be forbidden to amass private possessions of any kind. Indeed, they are not so much as to have private houses, but are apparently to live in a kind of perpetual garrison. The object of this provision is simply to prevent the growth of private interests on the part of the 'guardian,' which might conflict with entire devotion to the public welfare, and we may conjecture that it was suggested in part by the painfully familiar fact that even the Spartan, the most public-spirited of Greeks, usually showed himself shamelessly venal when placed in positions which gave him the chance to make his private market of the trust reposed in him. A similar object underlies Plato's daring attempt to abolish the private family. A private family he regards as a standing temptation to disloyalty on the part of the public servant to the public interest. As the late R. L. Nettleship has put it, Plato's objections to the family are explained by the associations of such words as 'nepotism.' We may add that he is alive to the truth expressed by the epigram that *un père de famille est capable de tout.* Moreover, with a splendid reliance on science, Plato thought it possible by scientific prevision to control the propagation of the human species so as to produce the best offspring. Hence his guardians are to regard the procreation of children as a public service, not as a private privilege. Marriages are to take place when the sagacious statesmen to whom the charge of them is committed, think desirable, and between such couples as they judge best. And Plato strongly maintains that in thus eliminating all elements of individual caprice from the union of the sexes he is not destroying but increasing the sanctity of marriage, by converting it into an act of public service. In the same spirit he forbids the whole system of 'home education.' Among his 'guardians,' no parents are to know their own children. All children are to be brought up together from birth, and to regard one another as one great family of which the whole elder generation are to be accounted the parents. In this way he thinks, by abolishing family selfishness, he will best promote the single-hearted devotion to the public welfare at which he aims. The State will be truly 'one,' because every man in it will call 'mine' just what every other citizen calls 'mine.'

These communistic proposals were already subjected to the unfavourable criticism of 'common sense' by Aristotle, and most modern students of Plato have hastened to echo Aristotle's objections. Yet we are perhaps inclined to unfairness of judgment by the fact that the conditions of family life among ourselves are so different from those which Plato has in view. It is natural to us to think of the family, when wisely administered, rather as the most valuable of preparatory schools of public spirit than as a nursery of selfishness, and to point to the fact that experience shows the moral effects of even an unsatisfactory home to be better than those of an 'institution' for the rearing of children. But it must be remembered that the basis of the modern Christian family is the existence of free cultivated and educated womanhood. In the Athens of Plato, the girls married young, they were apparently almost entirely uneducated, and were absolutely excluded from all the interests of life outside their husband's door. What kind of women this state of things produced, and how far they were fitted to be entrusted with the formation of a child's character in the first and most impressionable years of its life, we can learn from the picture of the Athenian women drawn by Aristophanes, their pretended champion. As Athenian society stood, Plato was probably not far wrong in his estimate of the moral effects of family life, and his proposals have all the merit of a serious attempt to recognise and remedy one of the gravest faults of the existing social order

(2) Plato strikes at the very root of the evil by his second proposal, which demands what we should now call the complete enfranchisement

of woman. Among the 'guardians' women are to receive the same training, bodily as well as mental, as men, and are to be employed indifferently with men in all the functions of a ruling class, those of active military service not excepted. There is, in fact, to be no sex disqualification for any form of public service. Plato's object in proposing thus to ignore sex as a fundamental fact of human nature is not by any means that of many modern 'feminist' champions, the extension of woman's 'rights,' or the gratification of her ambitions. It is the sphere of duties and burdens which he is anxious to enlarge; society, in his opinion, is, so long as women are excluded from active citizen life, voluntarily foregoing the services which it ought to receive from the female half of its members, and these services he proposes to recover. It may strike us as odd that Plato should not have assigned woman some specific sphere of social service, but should have preferred the paradoxical plan of introducing her as a rival of man in every sphere, even that of war. He seems to have been misled in the matter by the undue importance he attaches to the analogy to be drawn from the lower animals, in whom, as he observes, the difference between the sexes is mainly one of strength and size, and leads to no thorough-going differentiation of functions other than those immediately concerned in reproduction. In assuming that the same thing would hold good in the human species, Plato probably seriously underestimates the influence of sex upon human psychical development in general, just as in his proposal to suppress romantic personal love between man and woman he underestimates the significance of sexual emotion as a determining factor in the individual's life. This underestimation of sex as a spiritual force is, however, a fault which Plato shares not only with all Greek philosophy, but with the moralists of the Old and New Testaments, and it is the more excusable in him, since in the life that he knew by experience romantic love hardly existed except in the form of passionate friendship between youths. The homely Xenophon is the only 'Socratic man' whose writings show any appreciation of love between man and woman as we understand it. We must note, too, that owing to the communistic character of Plato's society, the economic objections which we feel to-day against the presence of women as rivals with men, *e.g.* in the work of a Governmental Department, have not to be considered by him, and also that the inevitable exclusion of women from many careers by the physical restrictions connected with the bearing and nursing of children would be largely done away with in his scheme by the abolition of the private home, and the transference of the duties of motherhood to the officials of the State nurseries.

Up to this point, Plato's ideal community may be said, with all its communistic elements, to be constructed on lines already familiar to contemporary students of the Greek city-state. The common education of the sexes, at least in bodily accomplishments, and the control of individual choice by regard for the needs of the community in the matter of marriage and procreation, were already in part realised by the discipline of Sparta. From Spartan practice, too, Plato may easily have derived the ideal of the garrison life he contemplates for his 'guardians.' Other ideas which he adopts were already 'in the air' in consequence either of the special social necessities of the fourth century, or of the speculations of the 'sophists.' The substitution of the trained professional soldier for the amateur citizen warrior has been noted as a characteristic of the Greek military history of the period following on the close of the Peloponnesian war. The abolition of slavery, silently presupposed by Plato, had been already vigorously advocated by more than one well-known 'sophist' on grounds which the conservative Aristotle finds himself forced to consider very seriously; the ideals of complete communism, free love, and emancipation of women are proved, not only by the tragedies of Euripides, but by the burlesques of Aristophanes, to have been quite familiar to the Athenian mind at the end of the fifth and opening of the fourth century. We might, in fact, say that Plato's object in incorporating so much of the current 'radical program' in his social scheme, is to rescue the new ideas from the ethical individualism out of which they had sprung, and to employ them as instruments for the intensifying and ennoblement of the old conception of duty to the 'city' as the supreme law of life which had been the foundation of the morality of historical Greece.

(3) The third of Plato's fundamental proposals, which he himself feels as the greatest paradox of all, definitely takes us beyond the limits of current Greek political thought, and amounts to the triumphant reassertion, in a transfigured form, of the Socratic conception of scientific knowledge as the true foundation of moral and political righteousness. Socrates had urged upon

the Athenian democracy, by familiar appeals to experience such as those preserved to us by Xenophon, the principle that no man is fit to administer in practice affairs which he does not understand; he had called, in effect, for government by experts in statesmanship.

This thought of Socrates, passed through the mind of Plato, reappears in the demand that the State shall be governed by 'philosophers.' Society will never be well ordered until kings become philosophers or philosophers kings. In other words, the highest intellect and the profoundest science are to find their proper employment in the direction of public life. The great curse of his own time, Plato thinks, is to be found in the existing divorce between science and statesmanship, a divorce which does no less injury to science than to government. Accordingly he proposes that a second selection shall be made from the ranks of the 'guardian' class, at the close of the first education, and on the verge of manhood. The selected few, who are to be the future rulers of the community, will be those who are distinguished alike by special intellectual capacity and peculiar moral nobility. They are to receive a thorough training in all the existing branches of exact science, passing from Arithmetic, through plane and solid Geometry, to theoretical Astronomy and Harmony, attention being throughout specially directed to the recognition of the fundamental principles, and the logical interconnection upon which the unity of the different 'sciences' depends. For this training Plato allots ten years of life, from twenty to thirty. All that is learned in these years is, however, a mere 'prelude to the strain' which is to follow. From thirty to thirty-five the statesman is to be occupied with the crowning study of Dialectic itself, by which he is finally prepared for the supreme vision of the 'Good.' At this point his speculative progress is to be interrupted; he is to be forced, as Plato puts it in one of his most famous apologues, to descend again into the 'cave' of error and confusion from which science has gradually delivered him, and to impart the results of his enlightenment to those who are still bound and in darkness. In other words, the lover of wisdom, arrived at the period of intellectual maturity, is to be taken from his studies and set to the hard work of governing men. It is only at fifty, after fifteen years of active public service, that he is to be dismissed to spend the remainder of his days in purely speculative contemplation of the 'Good,' and its offspring, the system of the ideal norms and concepts of science.

It is in this insistence upon the conjunction of the highest speculation with the management of practical affairs that Plato is most strikingly at variance with the views of his great disciple Aristotle. In Plato's ideal community there was to be no group of mere abstract thinkers devoted solely to the pursuit of the 'theoretic' life. He has nothing of the spirit of intellectual disdain for active affairs which led Aristotle to deny 'practical activity' to God, and to banish it from the life of the ideally 'god-like' man. It is pretty safe to assume that he would have dissented vigorously from the estimate of Aristotle, and apparently of Hegel, who seem to regard the mere student of metaphysics as the highest type of human being, since he is quite explicit on the point that the philosopher, as we know him in everyday experience, is as far from being what a philosopher might and ought to be, as the king of current politics is from being the true and ideal ruler *secundum artem*. We do Plato the gravest of wrongs if we forget that the *Republic* is no mere collection of theoretical discussions about government, and no mere exercise in the creation of an impossible Utopia, but a serious project of practical reform put forward by an Athenian patriot, set on fire, like Shelley, with a 'passion for reforming the world.'

The Platonic conception of a community ruled by men with a great philosophy of human nature, and divested, by their position in the social system, of any private ties which might lead to personal interests other than the one interest of getting their work for society well done, has often been compared with the theoretical constitution of the Catholic Church. Plato's rulers would, however, be saved from most of the temptations which have proved fatal to Catholic ecclesiasticism, partly by the frank recognition of science as the foundation-stone; partly by the provision that every 'guardian' is normally to beget children for the State—a regulation which would make the growth of 'other-worldliness' and the ecclesiastical conception of the 'spiritual' life almost impossible; partly also by the prohibition to possess private property which excludes anything like the formation of a clerical order with material interests of its own opposed to those of the 'lay' State.

Plato follows up his picture of the ideal State, in which life is absolutely swayed by devotion to an enlightened ideal of public good, and of the type of man in whom this principle finds its fullest expression, the philosopher, by a sketch of a number of inferior communities and corresponding inferior individual characters in which various degrees of divergence from the ideal are exhibited. These are so arranged as to form a series of successive degenerations from the ideal type, caused by increasing departure from the principle of the due subordination of the lower to the higher alike in the community and in the individual soul. At each fresh stage in the descent an increasingly unworthy class in the state or element in the soul usurps the predominant position, until the series closes with the mastery of state and of soul by their absolutely worst elements, and the consequent subversion of all real political and moral life. At the head of the scale stands the ideal community which we have described, and which may be called indifferently an 'aristocracy' or 'rule of the best,' or, in the case in which there is only one such pre-eminently best man in the whole society, a 'monarchy.' Similarly the ideal type of man who is the product of this society and gives it its peculiar tone, may be called not only the 'philosopher,' but also, as we have seen, the 'king' or 'kingly man.' (One may compare, and contrast, Carlyle's favourite conception of the king by God's grace as the 'man who can.') In the actual world, however, this ideal, if realised at all, could not be realised permanently; there is an element of imperfection in the actual which must inevitably lead to degeneration. The particular cause of decline in national and individual character is found by Plato in ignorance of the laws of heredity. Sooner or later our 'guardians,' being after all fallible, will beget children out of due season, and with the advent of this inferior generation to power the fall of society will begin. The first symptom of decline will be the neglect of education. First, the culture of the mind will be neglected for that of the body. Physical force, military prowess and skill, will come to have the preference over wisdom. Our State will be ruled by soldiers, and organised rather for war than peace. There will still be outward loyalty to the laws and institutions of a better age, but they will not be really understood, and the desire to amass personal riches will grow up among the 'guardians,' who will, however, in respect for the old traditions, gratify their growing avarice at first quietly and by stealth. The ruling spirit of such a State will be personal ambition and love of distinction, on which grounds Plato calls it a 'timocracy.'

The details of the description show that the instance of such a second-best society which he has in mind is contemporary Sparta. Such as is the 'timocratic' State is also its characteristic product, the 'timocratic man.' He is a man in whom chivalrous high spirit no longer takes the second place in the control of life, but becomes the ruling passion, obedient to law and the magistrates, but consumed by ambition for personal distinction to which he lays claim primarily on the ground of his merits as a soldier and sportsman. In mature age he will be liable, for want of a sound rational estimate of the various goods, to grow over-fond of money. Such a character is often found in the aspiring son of an excellent father who, living under an imperfect constitution, has avoided seeking public distinctions, and so come to be put down by the unwise as a creature of poor spirit.

A further decline is to be found in oligarchy. In an oligarchy, *i.e.* a constitution based upon property qualifications, wealth is treated as the chief good and poverty as disqualifying a man for public life. A man's worth is measured by his property, and there are thus always two parties in the State—the rich and the poor, the 'haves' and the 'have-nots.' In an oligarchy we find, what was absent from the 'timocracy,' a class of persons who have been permitted to alienate their property and become paupers, and a corresponding class of the 'rich' (millionaires we should now call them), who have acquired the alienated wealth. And both classes, Plato contends, are spiritually alike in rendering no real public service in return for their position in the State, in being drones in the national hive. The possibility of this development is already contained in the greed for wealth which was present, though concealed, in the 'timocracy'; only the law permitting complete alienation of patrimonies is needed to make the possibility into an actuality. If we ask what communities Plato has in mind in this description, it would be most natural to suppose that he is thinking of great commercial cities like Corinth, the Venice of ancient Hellas. The 'oligarchical man,' common in every society but predominant in such a one as we have described, is the man in whom the command of the soul is given over to the lower desires, though those desires are as yet gratified in a cold-blooded and calculating way. He is the man who makes it his highest good to command the things which money can buy, and the money which can buy them. His maxim is to make a profit out of everything, and to work hard and deny himself the full indulgence of his appetites, in order to be sure of getting his profit. Education he naturally despises; honesty he values in general as the 'best policy,' but his real opinion of it is betrayed when he gets the chance to make a dishonest profit with impunity, *e.g.* as a fraudulent trustee. We might liken him to the first generation of an American millionaire family. Plato thinks this type of character very common in the sons of ambitious 'timocratic' men whose schemes have failed and landed their authors in poverty and obscurity.

One remove further from the ideal 'government by the best' stands the democracy of which Plato's own Athens furnishes him with the spiritual type. Plato's judgments on democracy and all its works, though most illuminating, are always bitter to the last degree. He can never forget that it was not a 'tyrant' or an 'oligarchy,' but the restored and triumphant democracy, that took the life of Socrates, and it may be also that his kinship with Critias and Charmides biassed his judgment more than he knew. At any rate, he always speaks of democracy (which to the Greek ear, be it remembered, is synonymous with 'government by the poor, or non-propertied classes') much as Dr. Johnson was accustomed to speak of Whiggery, or Burke, in his evil days, of Jacobinism. It is the 'negation of principle,' the constitution under which no qualification of any kind, neither wisdom nor prowess nor even a 'stake in the country' is required of the ruler, but under which all men are free and equal, and one man is held about as fit to discharge any public function as any other. Nietzsche's epigrammatic description of modern democracy, 'one flock and no shepherd,' exactly reproduces Plato's verdict on the democracy of the ancient world. The democracy, he says, is not so much a constitution as an emporium of constitutions, with a dash of all of them in it. Every true democrat is allowed to do pretty much as he likes; if he likes, he may obey the laws; if he would rather break them, he is free to do it. He is under no legal or moral obligation to serve the public, but may please himself about it. He may conceivably get into trouble with the law and be sentenced to death or banishment, but as it is no one's business in so free and independent a community to enforce the laws, he can still walk the streets as safe as though he were a 'spirit' invisible to the officers of justice. In a word, the first principle of democracy is that there should be *no* selection of the 'fittest' to govern, for all are equally fit by nature, and this is why the outward sign of an ancient democracy is the use of the lot in appointing public officials. The historical transition from the oligarchy of wealth to such democracy, Plato thinks, might be prevented if the oligarchical State were wise enough to check the growth of the discontented class of 'have-nots' by abolishing legal remedies for breach of contract, and thus compelling the speculative financier to do business at his own risk. The oligarchical rulers, however, are careful not to take this step, since it would be opposed to their own ambition to accumulate wealth at their neighbours' expense. Consequently, the class of the dispossessed becomes daily more numerous, and it needs but some slight external occasion to reveal their own strength to them and to set them on deposing their masters. The 'democratic man,' whom we may often find in the son of a money-loving father who has been initiated by companions into the pleasures of profligacy and has learned to rebel against the paternal parsimony, resembles the democratic State in having no fixed principle of subordination of lower to higher within him. He makes no selection between different impulses to action; he is for gratifying each and every mood as it arises, and for so long as it persists, is 'everything by turns and nothing long.' At one time he is a profligate or voluptuary, at another he may take a fit for athleticism and the strenuous life. He may even, for a while, play the philosopher, but only so long as the mood lasts and its novelty amuses him. He is, in fact, the living embodiment of that shallow versatility which Plato dreaded for his 'guardians,' a consummate *poseur* to whom life is one long and diversified stage-play. Of course, while Plato's description hits off many of the besetting weaknesses of the Athenian character, we must remember that it is satire, and not sober history. To take it as an uncoloured account of Athenian life would be like taking Burke's anti-Jacobinical tirades as a faithful picture of France under the Directory, or Berkeley's caricatures in *Alciphron* as a true picture of the aims of eighteenth-century Deism.

Even in this lowest depth of social chaos, however, there remains a still lower depth. In 'tyranny,' *i.e.* the unfettered arbitrary rule of a single despot, we have passed beyond the mere absence of any principle of the choice of the fittest to rule to an actual choice of the unfittest. The organisation of a tyranny is a sort of infernal parody of that of a true 'aristocracy,' as the Middle Ages believed that the organisation of Hell was an infernal parody of the angelic hierarchy of Heaven. The worst and most dangerous villain of the community bears sway, relying on the physical force of picked bands of ruffians who come nearest to himself in criminality, and the best and most law-abiding citizens are massacred or exiled or frightened into submission. (Compare Shelley's picture of Anarchy enthroned in the palaces of England as 'God and King and Law.') In tracing the way in which such a tyranny may arise from a previous democracy, Plato is guided by the thought which has been frequently expressed in later times, that unrestrained democracy has a natural tendency to generate lawless military despotism. The details of his imaginary narrative are drawn from recollections of actual Greek history, the examples prominent in his mind being manifestly the career of Pisistratus at Athens and, perhaps, that of the elder Dionysius in Sicily. The 'tyrant' begins, like Cæsar in Rome, as an extreme demagogue, the champion of the proletariat against the well-to-do bourgeois. When once he has begun to shed innocent blood in his career as demagogue, his fate is sealed. He must either be destroyed himself, or make himself master of the lives and liberties of his fellow-citizens. So he appeals to his partisans for an armed bodyguard, (this point is clearly taken from the history of Pisistratus), and thus declares open war on the constitution. The rest of the story is a tale of steady moral deterioration. By degrees the tyrant is driven to kill or banish the best of the citizens, to distrust the advice of those who are left, to surround himself with foreign mercenaries and emancipated slaves, on whom he is forced to depend but whom he cannot trust. His whole life henceforward, though apparently one of prosperity and unlimited power, is secretly one of utter suspiciousness, helplessness, and misery. (This part of the picture shows signs of being specially drawn from the actual history of Dionysius I., of whose terrors and precautions against treachery even on the part of his own family so many stories are related by later writers.) Thus experience confirms the verdict of philosophy that the tyrant's life is really the most miserable of all. The 'tyrannical man' is, in similar fashion, the man in whom the 'democratic' gratification of all impulses as they arise has given place to the complete domination of the soul by some one base and criminal lust to the indulgence of which the man's whole life is sacrificed. In such a man, as in the tyrannically governed city, we see once more the selection of the least fit, the worst and vilest element in character, to have the supreme direction of conduct. What the misery of such a life is we may understand when we reflect that it is one of continual remorse and growing slavery. All that is best in such a man must be in revolt against the life he is leading, and the symptoms of this revolt are hard to suppress. Hence, in his calmer moods, he is a constant prey to remorse, self-disgust, and the pangs of guilty conscience. *Virtutem videt intabescitque relicta.* And, since the criminal appetite becomes ever harder to satisfy as it grows stronger and more insistent, he is hurried on from sin to continually fresh and worse sin, to be followed in turn, unless conscience is wholly dead, by worse terror and remorse. Such men are found in all societies among the ranks of the 'criminal classes,' but the type is not seen at its worst and wretchedest unless external circumstances enable the criminal to become an actual tyrant and to obtain the opportunity to execute his criminal will to the full. It will be remembered that it is for such 'tyrants' that Plato reserves the Hell of his eschatological myths. Once more, of course, we must not take the idealised picture for an historical estimate of the character of the actual 'tyrants' of the monarchical age of Greece. The nearest approach actual Greek history affords us to the Platonic 'tyrant' must rather be looked for in the career of some of the despots who ruled in half-barbaric outlying districts in Plato's own and the immediately preceding age, such as Archelaus of Macedon or the half-mad Alexander of Pheræ.

In a later dialogue, the *Politicus*, Plato returns to the problem of the classification of constitutions, and presents a scheme which recognises a rather higher value in existing 'democracies' than the *Republic* allowed them. As in the *Republic*, he still holds that the ideally best form of government is that of the wise philosophic monarch, who can afford to dispense with a formal code of written and unchanging law because his insight makes him competent to deal with every situation for the public good as the occasion requires, independently of prescription; the worst that of the 'tyrant' who knows no law but his own caprice. But intermediate between the two extremes are two types of government: government by the select few, and government by the many. And each of these forms may exist with or without fixed laws, so that we get four intermediate types in all: aristocracy (in the sense of government by the few under a fundamental 'law of the constitution'); democracy with such a law; democracy without law; oligarchy (arbitrary government by the few). Plato's final judgment is that, in the absence of the philosopher-king, for whose living wisdom law is an imperfect substitute, democracy is the inferior form of government where there is a fixed fundamental law, but the better where there is not. Of the provisions of the *Laws*, Plato's latest work on political science, I do not speak, since his avowed object there is merely to provide a system which might be immediately workable for very average Greek settlers; and hence his abandonment of the demands for communism of goods, abolition of the private family, emancipation of women, and the rule of philosophers, must not be taken as a renunciation of his ideals, especially as communism is declared in the *Laws* itself to be the ideally better way, and the general political scheme of the *Republic* reiterated in the *Timaeus*.

CHAPTER IV

COSMOLOGY

I MAY conclude this sketch by an exceedingly brief *résumé* of one or two of the main principles of Plato's cosmology as given in the *Timaeus.* As we have seen, Plato holds that actual sensible fact, as it stands, cannot be the object of exact science; we must content ourselves, in dealing with the physical world, with 'probable opinions.' Thus the cosmology of the *Timaeus* is formally announced as being largely commingled with myth, and it is not always easy to say where conscious myth leaves off, and what Plato regards as at least a probable account of non-mythical fact begins, and it is not surprising that there should have been even in the Academy itself considerable variety of opinion as to Plato's real views about the physical world. For my own part, I deem it most desirable here to state what Plato says, without entering far into the interminable dispute as to what he means. The *Timaeus* is, in form, not only a cosmology, but a cosmogony.

It not merely describes the structure of the physical universe, but professes to tell the story of its formation. The sensible world, according to the narrative, is not eternal, for it is something which 'becomes,' *i.e.* it is subject to incessant change. It had therefore a beginning and a cause. This cause appears in the *Timaeus* as a personified deity, the *Demiurgus* or world-maker. The reason for the making of the world is to be sought in the goodness of its maker; being good himself, he desired to communicate his own perfection to something outside himself. Hence he fashioned the changing world of sense on the model of the unchanging world of eternal Ideas, as far as such a thing was possible. From the unity of this model Plato deduces the unity of the copy, the physical universe, and therefore pronounces against the doctrine of 'plurality of worlds.' But Plato goes still further; not only is the visible world one and not many, it is a living organism with a soul and a body of its own, a single 'animal,' embracing within itself all minor forms of animal life, just as its model the 'intelligible animal,' or 'Idea of animal,' comprehends in its logical extension all the varied 'types' of animal species. Plato now proceeds to describe the formation of both soul and body of the great world-animal. In both cases, the formation is not a creation out of nothing; what the Demiurgus does is to combine in fixed proportions and by definite law elements which are presupposed as already in existence. The 'soul' of the world is constructed from three elements, Sameness, Otherness, and an entity which is described as produced by a preliminary union of the first two. Here we seem to have a reference, in mythical form, to the three levels of cognition known to us from the *Republic*: apprehension of the immutable Ideas, 'opinions' about the incalculably varying world of existing fact, apprehension of the intermediate class of 'mathematical' objects. The body of the universe is composed of the traditional 'four elements' of Empedocles—fire, air, water, earth—but Plato is not content to accept these elements as ultimate and unanalysable. He makes a remarkable attempt to lay the foundations of a purely mathematical physics by reducing the differences between the 'elements' to differences in their geometrical structure. The molecules, as we should now call them, of the four elementary substances are made to correspond respectively to four regular geometrical solids: the tetrahedron, octahedron, icosahedron, cube. The sides of the first three of these solids can all be constructed by putting together right-angled triangles in which the hypotenuse is double of the shorter side; for the construction of the square face of the cube Plato employs four isosceles right-angled triangles. This difference in the character of the elementary triangles from which the regular solids are built up is employed to explain what Plato regards as the fact that fire, air, water are convertible into one another but not into earth. The mathematical analysis of matter into geometrical form reaches its furthest point where Plato explicitly identifies the 'matrix,' or 'substrate' of physical change, with space, thus anticipating the physical theory of Descartes, just as in his doctrine of 'reminiscence' he has anticipated the same philosopher's conception of 'innate ideas.'

By way of marking the superiority of soul over body, Plato asserts that the soul of the world was fashioned by the Demiurgus before its body, just as, at a later stage of the narrative, we find the human soul constructed long before the destined date of its incarnation in a human body. The soul, once formed, is then figuratively spoken of as being diffused throughout space in accordance with a mathematical series which is intended to express the relative distances of the various heavenly bodies from the earth, taken as the centre of the whole system. With the bringing into being of the orderly system of the heavenly bodies, time, regular measured duration, also begins to be. Into the details of Plato's astronomical system and the question of its relation to Pythagorean science we cannot enter in this brief sketch.

From cosmogony proper the *Timaeus* proceeds to consider the formation of the human soul and body. The 'immortal' souls of future human beings are fashioned by the Demiurgus himself from the same material as had previously been employed in the construction of the soul of the world; the two inferior 'mortal' souls, of which we have already spoken in dealing with Plato's psychology, are then fashioned and added to the immortal soul by the lesser deities, themselves the earliest of things created after the world-soul itself. The very interesting details of Plato's sense-physiology and psycho-physics we must once more perforce pass over.

On the many exceedingly difficult questions which arise when we attempt to interpret Plato's great cosmogonic myth I can only say one or two words. There has been a good deal of discussion as to whether the Demiurgus is to be thought of as a personal deity or as a purely imaginative personification of 'the good.' Perhaps the true answer is that he is neither the one nor the other. The sharp distinction which we possess, or fancy ourselves to possess, between the personal and the impersonal, can hardly be said to exist for any classical Greek thinker; the very language, in fact, has no term by which to express it. And again, the 'good' figures so manifestly in the *Timaeus* as the model contemplated by the divine artist in constructing his work, that we cannot without confusion of thought identify it at the same time with the artificer. (In the one sentence, the last of the dialogue, where according to some MSS. the identification is made, the word *ποιητοῦ* is pretty clearly a false reading for the *νοητοῦ* of other MSS., due probably to misunderstanding of the construction.) The natural inference from Plato's well-known view of soul as the origin of all movement would be that the activity of the Demiurgus is an imaginative rendering of the great thought of Anaxagoras, that it is mind that has set all things in order. To ask whether that mind is 'personal' is to commit an anachronism.

From the time of Xenocrates, Plato's immediate pupil, onwards, it has been a hotly disputed question whether Plato meant seriously to ascribe a beginning to the physical universe, or whether his account is only meant as a device for presenting a logical analysis of the physical world into its constituent factors under the guise of an imaginative fiction. The latter view was definitely accepted as correct by the whole Neo-Platonic school, who were anxious to find in Plato the Aristotelian doctrine of the eternity of the universe, and has perhaps, on the whole, found most favour with modern expositors. The former interpretation, according to which Plato is perfectly serious in ascribing a beginning to the universe, was, however, that of Aristotle, and was also defended by Plutarch in his very sensible essay on *The Formation of the World-Soul in Plato's Timaeus.* The reader must be left to come to a conclusion for himself by an independent study of the Platonic text, but I cannot forbear to express my own conviction that Plutarch is right in maintaining that the theory of the eternity of the world can only be read into Plato by a violent and unnatural exegesis which strains the sense of the most obvious expressions in the interest of a foregone conclusion. At the same time, Plato does not conceive of the world as having a beginning '*in time,*' since he expressly conceives of time as regular and measured duration, and as therefore coeval with the existence of the regularly moving heavenly bodies. What came before the ordered 'world,' according to his narrative, was a state of things in which there was nothing but confused and lawless motion. A comparison of the *Timaeus* with the myth in the *Politicus* with its alternate cycles in one of which God directs the course of the universe, while in the other it is left to itself and becomes in consequence more and more lawless, and verges closer and closer upon dissolution into chaos until its maker once more 'takes the helm,' seems to me, as to the late Dr. Adam, to suggest the conclusion that Plato, like some other thinkers before him, believed the history of the universe to be made up of alternate periods of decay and reconstruction, and that what we have in the *Timaeus* is a picture of such a period of reconstruction following on one of previous dissolution. If this is so, the materials of which the Demiurgus fashions his 'world' would be, to speak roughly, the ruins of a world that had gone before, and we should at once understand why it is the 'world,' and not the elements, or their constituent triangles, which is said to have had a beginning.

One comparatively minor question of astronomy

deserves a word of special notice, since it concerns Plato's claim to be reckoned among the 'Copernicans before Copernicus' of antiquity. Does Plato in the *Timaeus* so far anticipate Copernicus as to allow, like the Pythagoreans, of a daily revolution of the earth? The facts are these. It is universally recognised that the *Timaeus*, besides locating the earth in the centre of the universe, explains the alternation of day and night, and the paths of the sun and planets, in a way which implies the immobility of the central earth. Day and night are due to an actual diurnal revolution of the outermost heavenly vault, which carries round with it all that is contained in its compass. The apparent paths of the sun and planets are then resolved each into a combination of two circular factors: an axial rotation of each in the plane of the equator, and a motion of revolution peculiar to each planet, which takes place in the plane of the ecliptic, in the opposite sense to the daily revolution, and has a longer period, viz. the 'year' of the planet in question. This analysis would, of course, be ruined if we supposed the central earth to be anything but stationary. It happens, however, that in speaking of the position of the earth in the solar system, Plato employs an ambiguous and poetical word of which the literal signification is to be 'packed' or 'squeezed' against something, but which has also the acquired signification of confined movement in a narrow space around a thing. His words may be rendered in English in a way which preserves the ambiguity of the original text thus, 'earth, our foster-mother, which is *rolled* round about the axis that stretches from end to end of the all.' Now Aristotle quotes these very words, naming the *Timaeus* as their source, and adding the interpretation 'and moves' after the words 'is rolled,' as a proof that some thinkers had denied the immobility of the earth. Hence Grote has maintained that the *Timaeus* expressly recognises the diurnal rotation of the earth upon its axis, and that Plato has simply overlooked the inconsistency between such a rotation of the earth and the rest of his astronomy. So very glaring an oversight, however, seems so improbable, that it is much easier to suppose that Aristotle has been misled by Plato's employment of a rare and ambiguous word, or possibly, as was held by August Boeckh, that some of Plato's followers had already misinterpreted the text of the *Timaeus* in the sense which Aristotle puts on it.

It seems certain, however, that in his extreme old age Plato did modify his astronomical views in a way which implies recognition of the earth's mobility. Plutarch tells us twice over that Plato 'in old age' regretted having placed the earth in the centre of the universe, a position which should have been secured for a 'better body,' and he gives as his authority for the statement the unimpeachable testimony of Theophrastus, the successor of Aristotle, who had himself been a pupil of Plato. This accords excellently with a passage of the *Laws* in which Plato denies that the paths of the planets are really composite, and declares that each of them has, in spite of appearances to the contrary, a single simple and uniform motion. This, of course, implies that one of the two motions ascribed to each planet in the *Timaeus* must be an appearance due to the real motion of the earth. Whether Plato conceived of this motion of the earth, as the later Pythagoreans did, as one of revolution round a centre, or as one of rotation about an axis, and, in the former case, whether he thought with the Pythagoreans that the centre in question is a body invisible to us, or identified it with the sun, the data do not permit us to decide. In any case, it is interesting to see that Plato's thought on these matters was still progressive even in his later years, and it is instructive to observe that, like other astronomers of antiquity, he only reached the truth about the earth's mobility by ignoring the still more fundamental truth that all curvilinear motion is composite. If he in some sort anticipates Copernicus, he has no presage of the infinitely profounder thought of Galileo and Newton.

ANN ARBOR PAPERBACKS *reissues of works of enduring merit*